A STUDENT'S GUIDE TO STRESS MANAGEMENT

**Richard Parsons and
Karen Dickinson**

cognella® | ACADEMIC PUBLISHING

I0123742

Bassim Hamadeh, CEO and Publisher

Kassie Graves, Acquisitions Editor

Berenice Quirino, Associate Production Editor

Miguel Macias, Senior Graphic Designer

Alexa Lucido, Licensing Associate

Don Kesner, Interior Designer

Natalie Piccotti, Senior Marketing Manager

Kassie Graves, Director of Acquisitions and Sales

Jamie Giganti, Senior Managing Editor

Copyright © 2018 by Cognella, Inc. All rights reserved. No part of this publication may be reprinted, reproduced, transmitted, or utilized in any form or by any electronic, mechanical, or other means, now known or hereafter invented, including photocopying, microfilming, and recording, or in any information retrieval system without the written permission of Cognella, Inc. For inquiries regarding permissions, translations, foreign rights, audio rights, and any other forms of reproduction, please contact the Cognella Licensing Department at rights@ cognella.com.

Trademark Notice: Product or corporate names may be trademarks or registered trademarks, and are used only for identification and explanation without intent to infringe.

Cover image copyright © 2017 iStockphoto LP/Peopleimages.

Printed in the United States of America.

ISBN: 978-1-5165-1533-2 (pbk)

cognella® | ACADEMIC PUBLISHING

A STUDENT'S GUIDE TO STRESS MANAGEMENT

THE COGNELLA SERIES ON STUDENT SUCCESS

S tudent success isn't always measured in straight As.

Many students arrive at college believing that if they study hard and earn top grades, their higher education experience will be a success. Few recognize that some of their greatest learning opportunities will take place outside the classroom. Learning how to manage stress, navigate new relationships, or put together a budget can be just as important as acing a pop quiz.

The Cognella Series on Student Success is a collection of books designed to help students develop the essential life and learning skills needed to support a happy, healthy, and productive higher education experience. Featuring topics suggested by students and books written by experts, the series offers research-based, yet practical advice to help any student navigate new challenges and succeed throughout their college experience.

Series Editor: Richard Parsons, Ph.D.
Professor of Counselor Education, West Chester University

Other titles available in the series:

* *A Student's Guide to a Meaningful Career*
* *A Student's Guide to College Transition*
* *A Student's Guide to Self-Care*
* *A Student's Guide to Money Matters*
* *A Student's Guide to Communication and Self-Presentation*
* *A Student's Guide to Exercise for Improving Health*

ABOUT THE AUTHORS

I ncreased demands. Living with roommates. Exploring independence. New romantic relationships. Tons of opportunity. Academic life is full of new stressors—but stress doesn't have to be a bad thing!

A Student's Guide to Stress Management provides you with strategies to not only manage stress, but transform stress into an asset that will help you succeed in your academic career. This guide will help you develop a deeper understanding of what stress is, it's positive and negative effects on physical and emotional health, and how it's a natural, and at times, helpful, part of the college experience.

Accessible yet comprehensive, this guide will prepare you to navigate the stressors of academic life like a pro, transforming stressful situations into opportunities for growth and success.

A Student's Guide to Stress Management is part of the Cognella Series on Student Success, a collection of books designed to help students develop the essential life and learning skills needed to support a happy, healthy, and productive higher education experience.

Richard Parsons is a professor of counselor education at West Chester University and has over 37 years of experience in teaching counselor preparation programs. He has authored or co-authored over 80 professional articles and book chapters, and serves as the editor for the Cognella Series on Student Success. Dr. Parsons earned his master's and doctoral degrees from Temple University.

Karen Dickinson is an associate professor of counselor education at West Chester University. She is a certified school counselor with more than 20 years of experience serving as a counselor and elementary and special education instructor. Dr. Dickinson earned her master's degree in elementary school counseling from West Chester University and her doctorate degree in individual and family studies from the University of Delaware.

CONTENTS

Unit I: Stress: The Good ... the Bad ... and the Reality

Unit II: Demands ... Demands ... and More Demands

Unit III: Stress-Busting Tool Box

EDITOR'S PREFACE

T he transition to college marks a significant milestone in a person's life. Many of you will be preparing to live away from your friends and family for the very first time. Clearly this is and should be an exciting time.

It is a time to experience new things and experiment with new options. While the opportunity to grow is clear, so too are the many challenges you will experience as you transition from high school to college.

Research suggests that the first year of college is the most difficult period of adjustment a student faces. Not only will you be required to adjust to new academic demands but you will also have to navigate a number of social and emotional challenges that accompany your life as a college student. The books found within this series—*Cognella Series on Student Success*—have been developed to help you with the many issues confronting your successful transition from life as a high school student to life as a collegiate. Each book within the series is designed to provide research-based, yet *practical* advice to assist you succeeding in your college experience.

The current book, *A Student's Guide to Stress Management,* provides the reader with well-researched, practical advice in developing skills for stress management. As you will soon come to discover, while the topic is serious, the manner in which the information is presented is both engaging and directly applicable to your current life experience. The book employs case illustrations in a feature called "*Voices From Campus*" and opportunities to apply what you are learning in a feature called "*Your Turn.*" I know that you will find this, as well as the other books within the series, to be a useful guide to your successful transition from high school to college.

Richard Parsons, Ph.D.
Series Editor

AUTHORS' PREFACE

AUTHORS' PREFACE

College applications, admissions tests, waiting for letters of acceptance, or perhaps reading letters of rejection are stress-filled experiences. But you knew that!

What you may or may not know is this stress doesn't end with the reception of your letter of acceptance or with the delivery of your financial deposit. While the specific types of stressors may change, the experience of stress will be one that you will carry throughout your life. Stress is part of our human condition and it will never end. In fact, as you will see in Chapter 2, you would not want it to end. The issue isn't how you gain a "stress free" life. The issue is how you best manage your stress so that it works for you, NOT against you.

In the chapters that follow you will learn about the plusses and the minuses of stress and the way it can and does affect each of us. You will be helped to begin to identify the unique opportunities to be encountered as a college student, opportunities that are inviting, stimulating, and yes, stress filled. Finally, as you read through the book you will discover strategies that not only will assist you in managing stress but also help you turn stress into an asset, one that supports your success in this new venture as a college student.

KD/RP

UNIT I:
STRESS: THE GOOD
... THE BAD ...
AND THE REALITY

WHAT IS STRESS AND HOW DOES IT AFFECT US?

Stress? Yeah, I know what that is. When you can't handle something and you are like freakin' out. Not me! I'm graduating in a month, already accepted to college. Okay, maybe I'm a little concerned about this roommate thing and the workload at college … so maybe a little … stressed?

S tress? The term is something with which we are sure you are familiar. We are sure that you have experienced stress and maybe could even describe a time when you felt it. What you may not realize is that we all experience stress, and we experience it daily!

So what does that mean? Well at minimum it means stress is part of life and living and that, in and of itself, it is not the evil thing we make it out to be. It also means that stress does have an effect on us, and under some circumstances that effect is not so good and can actually be quite harmful. So where do we go?

Like most things, a good place to start is to gain some understanding about the nature of stress, the causes of stress, the impact of stress, and the "what" you can do to manage stress so that it is not destructive to you. That's what this chapter, even this book, is all about!

1.1: What Is This Thing Called Stress?

Your body is at work every minute of the day, and when it reacts to a demand or a threat, the result is stress. Wait, let's think about that for a minute. Above we said that stress is something we all experience and we all experience daily. Well, if stress is our response or reaction to demands or threats, then we not only experience it daily, we experience all throughout the day. Think about it. You just ate a spicy taco. Guess what? No, not indigestion! Stress! Yep. Prior to eating, your gastric juices, your internal temperature regulation, your adrenaline levels, your metabolism, etc., were all operating at a particular level. Then, (and we are not sure why you would this) but then … you ate the TACO Diablo, and bingo, your body, or physiological systems, are all under threat. The introduction of this food has now placed a demand on your body to adjust and eventually return your body to its previously resting state. That … is stress!

Wait a minute, does that mean that every situation to which the body responds is considered stress-filled? Yep! And it is not just the "body." Every time your attention is re-directed, or your thoughts are challenged, or you mentally ask the question "what was that," you are experiencing stress. So the short story is that stress occurs anytime we are placed in a situation where we are forced or asked to physically or psychologically adapt.

Now, given the clear prevalence of stress in our life, how come situations that cause stress to one person don't cause stress to every person? Great question!

1.2: Stressors

As you read, stress is a response to a demand or threat. But what actually constitutes a demand or stress? I mean, if a tree falls in a forest and you are not there to experience it, are you stressed? Nope. Similarly, for us to experience stress the event must be recorded not only in our body, but also in our brains. It is the reaction of our body and the interpretation or meaning that we give to our experience of an event that determines if it is a demand or threat, or stress. Further, your perspective on whether the stress is positive or negative will make a difference in how you respond.

There are many different types of stressors including environmental, biological, thinking, and behavioral stressors. Environmental stressors are those factors or conditions in your physical environment that may place your body under a demand to adapt. Some of the dramatic stressors are things like natural disasters and pollution. But there are daily demands, including those experienced if you move from a classroom that is hot to one that is chilly. Those goose bumps and shivers are evidence of being physically stressed. There are also biological stressors. These may include having an illness or disability that somehow makes your daily activities more difficult to perform. We are sure you have had a day when you were attempting to take a test and you were at the beginning stages of a cold, or the flu … or a headache. These biological conditions placed an added burden that stressed you as you attempted to respond to the test. We invite you to consider what happens in Voices From Campus 1.1

VOICES FROM CAMPUS 1.1

I Just Won't Go!

I remember the day well. I was just starting to get notifications from the colleges about acceptances and I was so psyched that I was going to college and getting out of my house. The last few months had been hell—really uncomfortable between my parents and me. They kept harping on me about making good decisions and looking at finances when choosing where to go to school. I always wanted to go to State, and I know it is hours away from home and definitely costs more than what we have around here. But … wow, the campus was beautiful and I just knew it would be peaceful, in fact anywhere away from my hometown would be great! Then it all fell apart. My dad's company was moving and he wasn't going with them. He had no job, no income, and I couldn't go to my dream school. I couldn't believe he did this to me! It was too late to apply for scholarships and financial aid. I didn't even know if I could afford to go to a local college. Oh, and what the hell … I got mono. Sure why not really kick a person when he's down.

I felt like my world had come to an abrupt halt. I couldn't eat or sleep, and all I could think about was I would be stuck at home and that just couldn't happen. I felt cornered and didn't know what to do. To make it worse, my grades were starting to slip from my lack of concentration. Actually, I was beginning to not even care anymore. I started to think that maybe I just wouldn't go to college!

You may be thinking, "Wow … I can't control these things. I'm doomed!" Ah, remember that when presented with a demand to adapt (i.e., stressor) your view of that demand and the form of your adaptive response may produce a positive or negative outcome! Let's look at the other types of stressors before exploring different outcomes. The first two types of stressors, environmental and biological, are stressors we may not have much control over. However, the following two types of stressors differ in that we may be able to manipulate them to some degree.

Thinking or cognitive stressors occur when we encounter a mental challenge, something that requires us to shift focus or to engage in some mental process (e.g., remembering, problem solving, creativity) with which we were not currently engaged. Examples of this type of stress are taking a test or writing an essay for your college applications. But don't forget, since stress is any demand for adaptation, which in this case would be a demand for cognitive (mental or thinking) adaptation, playing a Madden NFL video game or Minecraft is also cognitively stressful.

The last category of stressor we'll call behavioral stressors. While it is somewhat artificial to separate behavioral from physical or cognitive, it helps to categorize them separately for purposes of discussion. So when you pull an all-nighter and thus do not get enough sleep, or overdo it at the gym, or smoke, or drink alcohol, you are engaging in behaviors that place demands on your body (and most likely your mind). Now we are aware that some of you may be thinking that using a bit of tobacco or alcohol can have a calming effect, a de-stressing effect. Perhaps that is what you "experience," but remember that introducing those chemicals into your body demands physiological adaptation and thus constitutes additional stress. We'll come back to this later in the chapter.

So if eating a taco, playing a video game, staying up later than usual are stressors, you can imagine what major life events are. Whether we call it a positive or negative life change, things like death of a loved one, getting married, graduating high school, and even going to college, require the demands for adaptation to be plentiful, and by definition then, so is the stress! Your Turn 1.1 is an exercise that invites you to reflect on your experience to stress and your reaction to it. Increasing your self-awareness will be an important step to more successfully managing your stress.

YOUR TURN 1.1

Identifying a Stressor

Directions: Stress and stress response is truly a personal experience. It is helpful for you to raise your awareness of stress in your life. As such we invite you to identify a stressor in your life from each of the different types of stressors. For each stressor you identify, consider the following:

Have you considered it a stressor before?
How do you deal with this stressor?
What are some possible outcomes if you continue to deal with it in the same way?
What are some possible outcomes if you choose to deal with it in a different way?

Regardless of the ability to control the occurrence of these stressors, we do have the ability to help shape how we handle the stressors. Many strategies will be explored later in the book; however, for now, let's look at how the body and mind are naturally programmed to respond to stress.

1.3: Physical Responses to Stress

When you feel threatened (and remember anytime you are required to adapt, it is a threat), your nervous system releases a flood of stress hormones that get the body ready for action. You know, the old "fight or flight" response. These hormones include adrenaline and cortisol that, among other things, increase your heart rate and make your senses keener.

This "fight or flight" response enables you to increase your strength and speed of reaction and enhances your focus. The positive impact of this arousal response is discussed in some detail in Chapter 2, but for now think about how these reactions may be helpful, protective, and even lifesaving in varying circumstances. Your Turn 1.2 invites you to reflect on your own "fight or flight" response.

YOUR TURN 1.2

Fight or Flight?!

Directions: Consider your body's response to stress in the following scenarios. What would the "fight or flight" response do for you?

1. You have 10 minutes left to finish a test and 25 more multiple-choice questions to answer.

2. You are getting ready to run the 100-yard dash. Your feet are on the starting blocks and the horn goes off indicating the start of the race.

3. You are alone and walking back to the dorm late at night and you hear a noise behind you.

4. You are the goalie in a hockey game and the puck is coming towards you.

You may have noticed that sometimes the "fight or flight" response could help you move towards a productive and positive outcome. That's true! Our stress response to a threat or demand may help us in a positive way. With only minutes to finish a test, our adrenaline levels could increase and help our focus to be sharper. Similarly, when faced with a hockey puck coming towards us, our response time may quicken as we protect ourselves and block a score from the other team.

Alternatively, our response to stress can have an adverse effect. Consider the student who is scheduled to make a speech next period in her public speaking class. She does not like to speak in front of large groups and starts to feel her muscles tighten and her heart beat faster. Her "fight or flight" response calls out to her to RUN! She escapes the danger that her body reacted to by skipping class and avoiding having to make the speech. Although she protected herself and momentarily decreased her stress, the consequences of skipping class and missing the speech may cause more stress in the near future.

Other physical and cognitive responses to stress may include chest pain, dizziness, memory problems, and the inability to concentrate. Stress is something that can really impact our ability to stay healthy and be productive!

1.4: Emotional–Behavioral Responses to Stress

While all demands for adaptation are stressful, some, like getting up to receive your trophy, are viewed as positive and desirable whereas others, such as standing up to hear the details of your sentencing at a trial, are seen and experienced as negative. Your perception of whether the stress you are experiencing is positive or negative will have an impact on your response to stress and its impact on you. As you will see in Chapter 2, positive stress can help to energize you and move you forward. However, perceiving stress as negative can not only slow you down, it can block you or actually stop you from reaching a goal. Remember the defeated thought at the end of Voices From Campus 1.1? We invite you to consider an alternative conclusion in Voices From Campus 1.2.

VOICES FROM CAMPUS 1.2

Roadblock or Curve?

So I can't go to college where I wanted to go. At first I felt like I had hit the worst roadblock in my life. What could be worse than having to stay at home and who knows what?! And then I realized ... wait, other people didn't even get in the colleges they wanted to and they're moving on, so stop your whining. I mean really, what if this isn't the worst thing that ever happened and it's a bend in the road, not a block in the road? What if going to school locally helped my parents with their financial strain and helped make me more independent? That's what I really want, right? I want to be independent and live my life—my choices. Maybe what I considered a roadblock is really just a curve in the road.

Emotional responses to stress may include moodiness, irritability, anger, and feeling lonely or overwhelmed. These emotional responses are not only uncomfortable but most often prove to be less than useful. For example, it is understandable that someone who is feeling overwhelmed and angry would have a hard time completing financial aid information before the deadline. To compound the situation, many who are experiencing the negative effects of stress then seek short-term solutions such as using alcohol, procrastinating, or withdrawing from others, which in turn not only increases the stress experienced, but also compounds the negative effects.

Wouldn't it be nice to simply bury our heads until this all passed by? Well—it won't. Further, attempting to ignore or hunker down when confronted by stress will only invite more serious, longer-term effects. Understanding what may happen if you do not deal with stress is the first step to learning how to best manage your stress.

1.5: Chronic Stress—What Happens in the Long Run

Remember when you read about the body's physical response to stress? Your muscles tense, your pulse quickens, and your brain uses more oxygen and its activity increases. In the short term, this can lead to productive behavior and even boost your immune system! However, if stress is chronic, those same hormones can suppress body functions and lower your immunity. When you experience stress over and over, the body doesn't realize the threat is over, and this can cause issues with your digestive, excretory, and reproductive systems. Ouch!

Your body does not have the ability to recognize the difference between daily stressors and life-changing events. Daily, routine stress may come from those responsibilities and pressures that you encounter throughout your normal day, things such as making sure you complete your class assignments, having enough hours at your job for covering college costs, and maintaining high grades. But there are other, more enduring forms of stress that might be experienced while attempting to adapt or adjust to a chronic illness or a traumatic event such as experienced at times of a natural disaster, war, or assault.

People under more enduring, chronic stress and those who have continued strain on their body over time, may encounter serious health problems, such as heart disease, high blood pressure, diabetes, depression, anxiety disorder, and other illnesses.

1.6: Stress—It's Not the Same for Everyone!

Stress is not the same for everyone. The ability to adapt to changing demands and even the perception and view of what constitutes a stress will vary from person to person and even from moment to moment, and these factors will affect the experience and the impact of stress. As we proceed through the upcoming chapters we will identify the factors, the approaches, and the personal styles that can help reduce not only the experience of stress, but also the potentially dangerous effects of stress. For now it is sufficient to say that we ALL can get better at coping with life demands and stresses and learn how to use them to our benefit. Interested? That's what the next chapters are for.

1.7: The Take Away

- Stress is the brain's and body's response to demands or threats.
- A stressor is a situation that puts a demand on the body or mind. Different types of stressors include environmental, biological, thinking, and behavioral stressors.
- Your perspective on whether the stress is positive or negative will make a difference in how you respond.
- Responses to stress can be physical, emotional, or behavioral.
- The longer the body responds to stress, the greater the chance of physical and/or mental illness.

YOU CAN'T AVOID STRESS, NOR WOULD YOU WANT TO

Don't you love it when people say to you, "Enjoy! These are the best years of your life"?

Best years? Yikes. How about all the deadlines, demands, and social pressures? How about the stress you feel?

Yep, it may be a surprise to some but the truth is that even young adults experience stress, real stress. But then you know that. You are stressed. You have to be. After all, you are human! And like it or not, stress is essential to the human condition.

As far as we know (and we do not have any direct experience with this), the only time you won't be stressed is when you are no longer alive and well. That excludes any belief in the "walking dead," who, from what we have seen on television, clearly remain stressed.

Stress is and should be part of living. While we may fantasize about being stress free, it is neither an achievable state nor is it a desirable state, as you will see.

2.1: Stress—Ouch!

To put it bluntly, stress, as you saw in Chapter 1, is bad for you. Or more accurately, can be bad for you. Stress can attack everything from your gums to your heart.

As we mentioned, stress, in the short term, can contribute to problems such as headache, stomach upset, sleep disturbances, short temper, and difficulty concentrating. And with chronic stress the impact can be even more destructive to your well-being.

Chronic stress can result in anxiety, insomnia, high blood pressure, heart disease, and a weakened immune system. And then to make things worse, some people attempt to deal with their stress using unhealthy strategies such as overeating, eating unhealthy foods (check those wrappers in your desk drawer), smoking cigarettes, or abusing drugs and alcohol.

Given that stress can generally make you miserable and be a challenge to your health and well-being, it would be easy to conclude that we simply need to avoid stress.

2.2: So Let's Just Go Mellow

So we are sure you get it, pressures and stress can build and it can really mess with your head and health. So we have an idea, let's all buy lottery tickets, win the "gazillion" dollars, and escape to some island where we can all be stress free!

Well, where do we start with the irrationality of such a fantasy? Perhaps the first thing we should attack is the chance of winning the lottery. But that is too obvious.

No, where we should look is at the incorrect assumption that winning the lottery and moving to an island would remove us from the experience of stress. If you want to do a little eye-opening research, check out "Here's How Winning the Lottery Makes you Miserable" at http://time.com/4176128/powerball-jackpot-lottery-winners/.

Lottery winners do not avoid stress, and in fact, they often find that their windfall in cash comes at quite a cost. But even this begs the point.

The fact is that any time we are presented with a condition or experience that requires us to make an adaptation, we are by definition placed under stress. So whether it is deciding on how to enjoy our "gazillion" dollars or attempting to find money for rent, stress is part of our life, part of living. While we can't live a stress-free life, our focus and goal can be on improving the way we respond to stress so that we may even use stress to our benefit.

2.3: Say What? Stress as Beneficial?

It is clear that stress can be bad for our health—both our physical and mental well-being. But what few people appreciate when they hear the term *stress* is that stress can actually be beneficial to our functioning. Honest! We know, this may be somewhat of an unexpected, even radical idea.

Radical? Perhaps.

True? Most definitely!

Typically when thinking about stress we think about the negative form of stress (which is typically called distress) and the negative impact of stress. But there is a second form of stress, called eustress, and it can be beneficial and can even contribute to our successful functioning. It is a form of stress most often associated with engaging with positive, pleasing demands.

Now, wait.

Before you jump to the conclusion that this is the rationale for your continuing to play your video games and thus wait until the last moment to attack that assignment, this is not exactly what we mean.

Eustress is not simply the avoidance of distress or the negative effects of stress. Eustress is the positive reaction one experiences when presented with a challenge. It is an experience of "excitement" and a reflection of our psychological arousal. For example, if you are one of those people who gets a rush out of riding a roller coaster or skiing a black diamond course or skateboarding or singing in public or (you can fill in your thrill-based activity here), then you know the experience of eustress.

During these activities your heart pumps fast, your muscles may tighten, and your concentration and focus are heightened. These are all our bodily reactions to the demands of the activity. These are all reactions to stress. Yet, they are perceived and experienced as that which is stimulating and life giving, something positive rather than the negative experience of stress encountered when we are being distressed. The following Voices From Campus highlights how a singular event, which in this case is receiving a lot of money, can be experienced as either distress (negative stress) or eustress (positive stress) and the effects that such a different perspective and experience can have on our well-being and functioning.

VOICES FROM CAMPUS 2.1

A Dream Turned Nightmare

I can remember it as if it were yesterday. I was entering my junior year at college and as a lark I bought a lottery ticket. You can't imagine the rush I got when I found out that I actually won 1.7 million dollars. I mean really, I'm 20 years old and now I'm a millionaire. How great is that?

Not great at all. First of all like an idiot I immediately dropped out of college. I am not sure what I was thinking other than I was going to live large. New car—maybe boat—lots of partying. Somehow the realities I was to encounter never came into that initial decision. It was within days that I began getting literally hundreds of calls a day asking for money. There were charities, investment schemes, political organizations, family members (some whom I never knew I had) and … oh yes, the Internal Revenue Service.

You would think that with 1.7 million—wait that was pre-taxes— with 925,000 dollars you would think a 20-year-old would be sitting pretty. I should have been, but I soon found myself being "worried" about money. Me! Worried about money! It was ridiculous. I was happy living in a one-room apartment off campus, eating Ramen noodles, and having one too many beers on Saturday. Now I sat, pretty much alone, in an upscale apartment, worrying about what I was going to do.

I can't blame the money, but I can tell you I wasn't ready to handle it and how I did was pretty darn upsetting to my health. I drank too much. I offended friends and family. I pretty much became a waste, blowing through almost $300,000 in nine months.

As depicted in the Voices From Campus in this chapter, stress, or if you prefer distress, can negatively affect each and every one of us. But when stress is encountered positively as eustress, it can improve our alertness, our memory, and our ability to perform and produce.

Stress Can Increase Our Focus

If you reflect on times in which you have been stressed you will most likely remember that your heart beat faster, your breathing rate escalated, and you may have become much more alert to what was happening around you. These reactions are all the result of your heightened cortisol and adrenaline levels. These changes represent carryovers from our earlier evolution and the need for self-protection and survival. These bodily and mental changes serve as preparation for "flight" or "fight" when confronted with danger.

While these changes still work in that fashion (i.e., to prepare us for flight or fight), we now know that when they are experienced at moderate levels they can improve both attention and cognitive functioning, even bringing them to optimal levels. Don't believe us?

Take a moment to step up and try it yourself by engaging with the following Your Turn 2.1.

YOUR TURN 2.1

Stress as Energizing?

Directions: Take a moment and identify a time in your life when something "big" was on the line. Maybe it was a major presentation in school or a project you were completing. Maybe it was a time of competition like during a major athletic event or performance in front of an audience. These situations are filled with pressure—stress. Now with the situation in mind ...

- Think about how you felt (you know, from "head to toe").
- Remember how you did.
- Now, regardless of how well you did, what would have been different if you simply did not care at all about the activity, the event, or the performance? Yes, you may not have had the butterflies in the stomach but how well would you have performed?
- Did your levels of extra adrenaline/cortisol serve you well?

Stress Can Increase Your Motivation

Have you ever seen an entire football team yell, cheer, and jump up and down in the huddle prior to going onto the field? Often they use those behaviors as a way of getting psyched. These actions, the yelling, the jumping up and down, the smacking on the shoulder pads, all serve to stimulate arousal, increase stress, and engage the mind and body in a way to maximize performance.

Think about your own experience. Have you had a deadline that served as a stimulus to get you focused and going on that which needed to be done? This is the potential motivational value of stress. But like most things there is a caveat we must offer.

When speaking of the motivational value of stress it is important to realize that it is not a straight, linear relationship where more is always better.

There is this very interesting "law" in psychology — the Yerkes–Dodson law. This "law" supports the notion that elevated arousal levels can improve performance. But just as the Yerkes–Dodson law suggests that elevated arousal levels can improve performance it also posits that while too little arousal will impede performance (really, who wants to do anything when zoning out?), too much arousal will overload the systems and interfere with performance. Thus the importance of learning how to manage stress so that it is not too much or too little but just right (guess we could call that the Goldilocks principle?).

For example, consider the football player who is so psyched and ready to go that he jumps off side or commits a penalty. Or how about the student (oops, maybe you) who is so over-hyped about his classroom presentation that he experiences brain-freeze, standing in front of class as if he were a manikin. Ouch!

Clearly, stress can stimulate and motivate effective performance, yet too much can be less than a good thing and counterproductive to our performance. As such, it is important to learn how to manage our stress response and perhaps learn to view stressful situations as challenges rather than unpassable roadblocks. This will be the focus of the upcoming chapters.

Stress Can Even Contribute to Your Self-Confidence

Learning to navigate stressful situations builds confidence and resilience. For example, Navy SEAL training introduces candidates to repeated exposure to stressful events. This practice of stress inoculation promotes the development of a sense of physical and psychological control thus helping the candidates believe in their ability to deal with future stressful situations.

Thus, when you not only experience stress but also realize that you have successfully navigated that stressful time, it will help build your resilience and enable you to engage stress in a way that works for you, rather than against you.

VOICES FROM CAMPUS 2.2

A Challenge and a Dream

As a senior finance major, the fact that I was suddenly thrust into managing my family's corporate empire was a challenge. Check that. It scared the piddle out of me.

I had just graduated from college when my dad decided to sell his company to a large corporation. The medical device that he invented and manufactured was now a hot commodity and he was selling his company for 2.5 million dollars. It truly was a rags-to-riches story and my dad deserved everything he was getting.

Sadly, my father passed away two months after the sale and only four months after my graduation. I am an only child and an orphan (my mom died when I was 13). And now, at the age of 21, I had inherited a couple million dollars.

The year following my dad's passing was a blur. Not much changed in my life. I stayed at our family home. I interacted with my friends and my cousins. But I pretty much experienced and managed my grief. As the pain of the loss began to subside, questions about what I was going to do, how I was going to live, and how I could best use the resources at hand all took center stage.

It was a lot, but I was really excited. I realized that I had many options, many paths I could follow, and while it was all a challenge, I felt it was a real gift. I found that my energy returned, my sense of creativity and drive increased, and I began to consult numerous professionals about business and philanthropy options. It was a time when life was good, and I only hoped my mom and my dad could understand how grateful I was.

2.4: Knowing This and That

By now you may be thinking, "So let's get this straight. Stress seems 'essential' for successful performance AND at the same time stress can kill you! Yep, thanks. Now I'm really stressed."

We sincerely doubt that what we told you was really new to you. We are sure that there are times when you have felt so stressed that you just wanted to bury your head or run away. You are probably quite clear about the negative impact of distress (negative stress). But if you reflect on your responses to the Your Turn 2.1 exercise, you hopefully now understand that there were times where stress (eustress) has worked for you!

Okay. So stress has worked for you. But we also know that there were times when stress took its toll on you. So how do you ensure that stress you experience is at a level that results in maximum productivity and functioning versus that which creates ill-health and dysfunction? While this will be something discussed throughout the remainder of the book, it is important to debunk one myth and misconception about stress and stressors.

When thinking about how to "manage stress," many people will simply suggest we need to learn to reduce our levels of stress by reducing the number of stressors. Now that certainly has an intuitive appeal and at some level makes sense. However this approach is what we call the "carpet the world to make it a comfortable place" mentality. That is if we could only make our world comfy, you know with minimal demands, minimal stressors, life would be super. Well, not only is such an approach not possible (remember life is by definition stress-filled) but it may not be the most productive approach since now we know stress can be beneficial. And the research highlights this point.

Surprisingly, it is not the number of life demands or stressors that is the primary factor in the "good" or "negative" impact of stress. As it turns out, it is more likely your "mindset," the way you "see" these demands, these stressors that serves as the primary determinant of whether the stress will be good or bad. Let's repeat that. It's not the number or frequency of life demands that determines the degree of negative stress ... it is how you perceive and react to these demands.

Wow! Think about it.

Perhaps you are a person who enjoys flying, so when you hear the rumble of the engines or experience a sudden dip due to air current it feels like a positive, exciting rush. Well next time you are on a plane look around. You will be able to see others, perhaps right next to you, who are white-knuckling through the entire flight. They are in the same plane, with the same engine noise and turbulence and yet the trip is anything but a positive, exciting rush. Same plane, same flight, same stressors and yet a different experience. Or consider the fact that there are some people who really get pumped and excited right before stepping on stage to perform in public. But that is not true for all. After all, there are some people who feel as if they are going to lose their lunch if they step on stage.

So is it really the demands of the situation we find ourselves in or the nature of the performance we are requested to do that serves as the source of this different response? Or is it that which the individual brings to the experience—the way they perceive the experience?

In Chapter 8 we will expand on this idea of the importance of "attitude" and "meaning-making" as an element which is pivotal to the degree to which life's demands are encountered as debilitating stressors or function as sources of stimulation and motivation. But for now, one simple finding is worth highlighting.

Researchers at Yale University have found that some people who appear to be most negatively impacted by stress are those who have a "stress is debilitating" mindset, seeing stress as bad; whereas those with a "stress is enhancing" mindset, those who encounter stress as an arousal experience, something that excites and energizes, more often experience stressors as facilitating to learning and performance. Where would you place yourself? (See Your Turn 2.2.)

YOUR TURN 2.2

Mindset

Directions: The following is an instrument created by neuroscience researchers for the identification of stress mindset. We invite you to respond to the questions posed. You may find it helpful to return to this assessment after completing the text.

Stress Mindset Measure (Crum, Salovey, & Achor, 2013)

Alia J. Crum, Peter Salovey, and Shawn Achor, "Stress Mindset Measure from Rethinking Stress: The Role of Mindsets in Determining the Stress Response," *Journal of Personality and Social Psychology*, vol. 104, no. 4. Copyright © 2013 by American Psychological Association. Reprinted with permission.

Items and Instruction for the Stress Mindset Measure—General (SMM-G)
Please rate the extent to which you agree or disagree with the following statements. For each question choose from the following alternatives: 0 = Strongly Disagree 1 = Disagree 2 = Neither Agree nor Disagree 3 = Agree 4 = Strongly Agree
1. The effects of stress are negative and should be avoided.
2. Experiencing stress facilitates my learning and growth.
3. Experiencing stress depletes my health and vitality.
4. Experiencing stress enhances my performance and productivity.
5. Experiencing stress inhibits my learning and growth.
6. Experiencing stress improves my health and vitality.
7. Experiencing stress debilitates my performance and productivity.
8. The effects of stress are positive and should be utilized.

Items and Instruction for the Stress Mindset Measure—Specific (SMM-S)
What is the primary source of stress in your life right now? In considering this particular stressor, please rate the extent to which you agree or disagree with the following statements. For each question choose from the following alternatives: 0 = Strongly Disagree 1 = Disagree 2 = Neither Agree nor Disagree 3 = Agree 4 = Strongly Agree
1. The effects of this stress are negative and should be avoided.
2. Experiencing this stress facilitates my learning and growth.
3. Experiencing this stress depletes my health and vitality.
4. Experiencing this stress enhances my performance and productivity.
5. Experiencing this stress inhibits my learning and growth.
6. Experiencing this stress improves my health and vitality.
7. Experiencing this stress debilitates my performance and productivity.
8. The effects of this stress are positive and should be utilized.

2.5: The Take Away

- Stress is part of life, it is evident that we are adapting to ever-changing demands.

- Stress can be destructive to our health and well-being, both at the moment and in the longer term.

- Stress, when experienced as positive, is physiologically and psychologically arousing and can contribute to our motivational level, our focus and memory, and even our self-confidence.

- Stress or the impact of stress appears to be less a function of the number of stressors experienced at any one moment, than how we interpret or give meaning to the stressors.

- For those with fear of flying and the experience of stress in flight, it is more about attitude than altitude, and this is true for all our stress experience—attitude and mindset define the experience.

I GOT ACCEPTED, HOW COULD THAT BE STRESSFUL?

I was like, blown away. Excited? Nope, insane!! Out of the four of us, I was the only one who was accepted. Whew, too cool.

The quote is from Amelia, a high school senior, who along with four of her best friends had all applied to the same Tier 1, very selective university. They all knew it was a long shot and they all had excellent fallback choices. But here it is. Amelia went to the mailbox and OMG … she got accepted. As she said … too cool!

By now you may have made many trips to the mailbox. Perhaps the sound of the mail truck marked an emotional high, or a near devastating low. The process of opening the box and wondering if you will find a thin envelope or one filled with information that announced your acceptance is clearly stressful. We know, you get it. Who wants to be rejected, especially with something so important?

But how about when the news is good? What a moment of joy! What a moment of relief!

It is and should be. But then why, following that moment or moments of celebration, does our old friend stress seem to return?

After reading the first two chapters you probably have a good idea how this could be possible. Being accepted into college is a wonderful accomplishment and it certainly deserves a sense of pride and celebration. However, as with any major life transition (even positive ones), getting into college can bring with it a great deal of stress. Getting a letter of acceptance, while certainly an opportunity to feel energized (eustress), can also be a stimulus to worry and to be concerned (distress). Acceptance into college can certainly be the opportunity to dream of increasing freedom, stimulating intellectual and social opportunities, or even just the benefits of getting out of "Dodge" (or West Chester, or Small-town, or ...). However, that same letter of acceptance can also be the first volley in what will feel like a major attack.

Reflecting on your acceptance you may begin to have doubts and concerns. Is it the joy of increased freedom or a fear of being on your own? You will be adjusting to different people and different ideas. Are these new opportunities seen as stimulating or threatening? And for those moving to campus, is it an opportunity to "escape" Small-town, USA, or the loss of that which is comfortable and familiar?

As suggested in Chapter 2 and will be expanded upon in upcoming chapters, it is *your view* of the demands you encounter, the stressors you navigate, that goes a long way in defining your response as either one of eustress or distress.

3.1: I Have Choices ... and Even That's Stressful!

We know that filling out those applications, writing essays, getting letters of recommendations, and meeting deadlines is a stress-filled experience. It is also stressful waiting for the letters of acceptance or rejection. Given the stress of applying for acceptance and waiting for the response, one might think that getting a letter of acceptance would be a relief. As noted above, it is ... for the moment.

Getting accepted, while a congratulatory experience, is also a request for a decision or decisions to be made. *Do you still want to go? Do you send that initial payment? Are there other options you should have considered?* Perhaps you can relate to the turmoil and nights awake, reflected by Raul in Voices From Campus 3.1.

VOICES FROM CAMPUS 3.1

Raul

My friends, my family, they really thought I was a nut. I mean for months I broke my back meeting with my counselor, engaging in career and college searches and self-directed exercises, then filling out all the paperwork and essays, and ... you get the picture. Kind of the same thing that everybody I know was doing, and it darn near killed us. So here I am sitting at the dining room table with my mom and dad, Aunt Maria, and my younger brother and sister. I kind of knew it was a letter of acceptance given the "thickness," but Mom wanted to film it, so everyone had to take up their positions.

As I unfolded the letter I saw only one word ... CONGRATULATIONS! Needless to say the table erupted, there were hugs and kisses and laughter. Truly it was something to cele-brate. So much so that Mom wanted me (us) to do it one more time just to be sure she had it on video.

Later that night as I was going to bed I placed the letter on my nightstand. As I tried to fall asleep I found myself excited like it was the night before Christmas kind of excited. So I decide to read a little bit, and that seemed to calm me down. So once again with head on pillow I tried to go to sleep and bingo!

It seemed like somebody had let loose a thousand and one ques-tions that flooded my brain. This is what I imagine those on the Titanic felt before it went down. Thoughts such as "What if this isn't the best major for me?" "Will I be able to get a job?" "How are we going to pay for this?" "Wouldn't it be better to work a year?" "OMG, what happens to Jen and I? I'll be 400 miles away!" became uncontrollable and flooded my brain. And these were just the tip of the iceberg (no pun intended).

I started questioning my ability to succeed, challenging the real value of college, and feeling pressured to be the first in the family to go to college and graduate. And the hits kept coming.

One letter, a wonderful letter of success, wrecked that night's sleep and at least a dozen more that followed. Whew. I never thought getting accepted into the college of one's choice would be so painful, so disruptive … so stressful.

While the reception of a single letter of acceptance is something to celebrate, it is also something that invites concern, worry, and stress. Now what happens if one receives more than one letter of acceptance? Clearly, such an experience should be affirming. I mean "you are in demand"!

One of the unique challenges now confronting you as you ponder the multiple offers that you have received is that now you must make a decision. Which one of the various paths will you take? It is a big and stress-filled decision, and to make matters even more difficult it is a decision that needs to be made in short order. After all they will not hold the spot forever.

The questions that may invade your moment of celebration might look like those experienced by Raul (see Voices 3.1), but even if you are not questioning your decision to go and all that comes with it, you will be confronted by the decision, the choice of … go where? Regardless if it is one letter of acceptance or 20, a decision to say "yes" to a college's acceptance is a major life-changing decision, and that is stressful.

Thankfully, you don't have to make such a decision on your own and in isolation from support and assistance. There are those who can help and steps you can take to reduce the debilitating effect of stress. One strategy would be to spend time with your counselor, your parent, your older sibling (if you have one) and try, with their assistance, to think about the pros and cons (or if you prefer benefits and costs) that going to college offers and, in the case of multiple acceptances, which college has the best ratio of costs to benefits. You may find it helpful to visit or revisit the school or schools. This time, however, rather than being in awe of the stadium, the library, and the classrooms, find a couple of students, preferably those who are enrolled in the major you have chosen, and/or a professor in your chosen field. Ask them about their experience. Invite them to share what it is, exactly, that they like and find life-giving at that school.

It is important to know about the credentials of the professors, the job placement record for the school, the status and prestige of the school, and even the support services that are available. However, remember that you will spend the major portion of your life on this campus for the next four or five years, so it is important to find out about how the campus is experienced as a place for growth and joy. In talking with the students, ask them if they would make the same choice if they could do it over again. Respectfully ask the professor if she truly enjoys and feels the campus stimulates and enlivens her personally and professionally. The more data you collect, the more information you can weigh, and then the more informed your decision will be.

This sense that you are making a reflective, data-based decision will not only reinforce the feeling that the decision you are making is the right one, but will increase your sense of control and empowerment and therefore reduce the anxieties and stress you may be experiencing.

Reduced stress, at least in relationship to making the initial decision, but wait … there's more to come. (Sorry!)

3.2: Okay, So I Have Decided

Whew, finally the deposit has been sent and my future is sealed. What? My future is sealed!

Stop … take a breath!

Yes, a decision has been made and it was an important one, but your fate, your future, has not been sealed. This has been a major step, a major accomplishment, but it is only one of the many opportunities you will have to give shape to your future. So for the time being relax and smile. You're in!

Okay—enough smiling and relaxing.

College is a different world, with different experiences (see Chapter 5). These new experiences will be accompanied by different demands and different needs to adjust and to adapt. Going to college is an introduction to exciting new opportunities, new people, new places, and the chance to go out on your own. The important word in the previous sentence is … NEW!

It is the new-ness of these experiences, even though they are positive and desirable, that will require adjustment, adaptation—therefore, by definition, STRESS.

3.3: What Types of Adjustments?

College life and the college experience are truly unique. It's a different world with many new opportunities and demands, all of which will at least initially pose a challenge and provide some stress. Now we are not just talking about the academics, or even adjusting to a new social environment with perhaps a different and diverse set of social opportunities, but even the small stuff like getting your laundry done, commuting versus being a resident, to say nothing of the endless desserts that greet you at the breakfast, make that lunch, no dinner tables.

But the one really big difference and perhaps significant change in your life will be that you are going to be treated as an adult rather than as a child. Think about that for a moment. That sounds good, and it is. One of the significant changes you will encounter as a result of this role redefinition is that there will be a lot less handholding, structuring, reminding, etc., and much more expectation of you doing "it" on your own.

Almost overnight you will find that rules have changed, and this is good. But the change, by definition, is stressful. You will experience new freedoms, freedoms to pick your own schedule, skip a class, choose from a buffet of more or less healthy foods to eat, and even lay in bed without someone banging at your door telling you that you will be late. But freedom comes with consequences and you will not be spared those. This point is certainly highlighted by Kasha in our Voices From Campus 3.2.

VOICES FROM CAMPUS 3.2

Kasha

Looking back I really feel foolish. I used to complain about all the responsibilities my parents threw on me and the fact that they were always in my business or harassing me about schedules and things that I needed to do. Wow!

By the end of my first month on campus I was praying that some-body would push me, remind me … even harass me. Really.

Whether it was simply staying on top of my assignments, figuring out a plan for studying, or even, and I know at 19 I shouldn't say this, but even waking up, the fact it was all up to me gave me too much room to mess up. And OMG, did I ever.

The idea of getting out my house and living on my own was exciting and something I really couldn't wait to do. The reality was a little different than the dream. Don't get me wrong from day one after saying good-bye to my parents I really got into life on campus. I made a bunch of new friends and had this "freedom" to party or do what I wanted to do or not do anything I didn't want to do, and the various opportunities and possibilities were really great. But that same freedom and my choices during that first month really revealed that I had some growing up to do.

It was simply too easy to put off the things I really needed to do and I had no one up my back to push, or direct … or help me. Initially it felt like it was now all up to me. Thankfully, I soon found out that there were people on campus, and of course my parents, who not only accepted that this was a time of adjustment and thus they gave me a little slack but also provided me with the support and guidance that I needed to get more control over my life and this college experience.

It took the best part of that first semester, but I understand that the freedom and autonomy I am experiencing brings with it a responsibility to choose wisely. I am sure it is a lesson I will continue to learn.

While some consequences are mild inconveniences like the added 15 pounds that come as a result of unlimited desserts, there are others with more significance such as a grade reduction for a late paper or a mistake in your scheduling that resulted in you missing a necessary prerequisite course. These can be more costly. Navigating this freedom is a wonderful opportunity and similarly a bowl full of stress.

Luckily, your freedom and the choices you have to make are not without support and resources. TALK! SHARE! ASK! SEEK GUIDANCE from your parents, older siblings, high school counselors, and counselors and freshman orientation staff on campus. There are resources that help you navigate the wonderful possibilities, but it is your choice to decide if and how to use them. And while you are still celebrating the wonderful news of acceptance, it may be useful to begin that dialogue now as a pre-emptive attack on the campus challenges and stress.

Interview those who have successfully navigated that first year on campus, gather notes, and learn from their experiences. Trust us, it can help! Your Turn 3.1 provides a list of the topics that you may want to consider in gathering the data necessary to reduce your stress and increase your success that first year.

YOUR TURN 3.1

Learning From the Experience of Others

Directions: While each of us will experience college differently, many of the challenges we will encounter are the same as those successfully navigated by people we know. We can learn from their experience. The following invites you to interview your teachers, counselor, parents, older siblings, and friends who have successfully survived ... make that "thrived" ... through their college days. You are then asked to take that information and develop a plan of attack that will help you reduce the needless stress that may be encountered while entering this new world.

Area	Question/Challenge	Recommendations	My Plan
Academics	1. How did you manage the increased workload?		
	2. Any hints about writing papers?		
	3. Is there a way to get a heads-up about professors or specific classes?		
	4. Is there one thing that you wish you did more of or maybe did less of that would have improved your grades and achievement?		
Campus / Social Life	1. What were the major challenges you experienced as a campus resident (or commuter)?		
	2. What about joining organizations including frats or sororities?		

	3. Any suggestions on services I should connect with?		
Daily Life	1. (For campus resident) Biggest downside of living away from home?		
	(For commuter) Biggest challenge of living at home and trying to adjust to college?		
	2. What did you wish you knew how to do (e.g., budget, plan, laundry, manage time, etc.) prior to starting college?		

3.4: From Distress to Eustress

As noted in Chapter 2, our arousal response when moved from our "comfort zone" and confronted with a demand for adaptation can be seen and employed in a way that truly serves our needs and desired direction. Under these conditions the stress we are experiencing is positive. It is eustress.

Remember that eustress is fundamental to our experience of excitement. Eustress energizes us, contributes to our eagerness, it can even serve as a base for our sense of thrill. In essence, eustress serves to provide the energy and readiness we need to respond to the challenges experienced at a particular moment and to maintain that energy as we grow in confidence and efficacy.

So perhaps your first challenge, now that you have been accepted, is to identify those demands that resulted from being accepted into college and turn that which is distressful (distress) into that which is exciting and energy producing (eustress).

A major determinant of whether one experiences a challenge as distress or eustress is the perception or view that they bring to the situation and the degree to which we feel in control and capable of responding to the demands of this new situation. Thus, getting a letter of acceptance can be an invitation to dream of increasing freedom, stimulating intellectual and social opportunities, or even just getting out of "Dodge" (or West Chester, or ?). But that same letter of acceptance can be an invitation to the nightmare of being on your own (versus increased freedom), being challenged by engaging with different people and different ideas, and not getting out of "Dodge" but rather moving away from the comfort of friends and that which is familiar. It is truly a matter of how you "see" it and whether you see yourself as capable of making the needed adjustments.

While we will discuss more specific strategies on how to move from distress to eustress in upcoming chapters, for now we invite you to 'take your turn" (Your Turn 3.2) as a way of increasing this moment of celebration while reducing needless distress.

YOUR TURN 3.2

From Distress to Eustress

Directions: So the letter or letters of acceptance are opened and proudly displayed. Let's take a moment to scan the degree to which your thoughts have turned to the demands that now IMMEDIATELY confront you, along with the degree to which these are experienced as distress or eustress.

Below you will find a list of things students have told us that they felt that they needed to address once accepted. Identify those that apply to you and specify if you experience these as "burdens" (distress) or "points of excitement" (eustress). Talk with your parents, your peers, and your counselor about ways to benefit from those that are energizing and reframe those that are distressing so that they energize, not burden, you.

Impact of Being Accepted	Eustress (E) or Distress (D)	Plan of Attack: If Eustress, how will you use the energy? If Distress, how can you address the challenge in a way that reduces the stress or even redefines it as positive?
I was accepted but my best friend was not.		
I didn't get my first choice and my friend did.		

Everybody is asking questions about why that college, why that major, and giving "advice."		
My parents want to post it on FB, they are super proud.		
Need to thank (counselor, teachers).		
Waiting to hear from my advisor on course selection.		
Wasn't my (parents', counselor's, teachers') first choice.		
Impact on current relationships (especially boy/girl friend).		
How do I keep motivated to keep up with assignments now?		
What will I need to get? Take? (if living on campus)		
Deposit is due.		
Tuition is a lot of money.		
Questions—Will I fit in (have the right clothes, style, etc.)?		
(Other challenges you feel at the moment.)		
(other)		
(other)		

3.5: The Take Away

- Being accepted into college is a wonderful accomplishment and it certainly brings a sense of pride and celebration, it also marks a major life transition and that is stressful.

- Acceptance into college invites us to not only "rethink" what we have done, but also ponder and question what it is that we are doing and where we are going, and both of these can be stressful.

- The acceptance into college can stimulate distress or the joy, excitement, and energy that define eustress. It is a matter of perspective.

- While there will be many changes and new experiences, the one perhaps most liberating and yet more stressful is the freedom you will experience and the fact that this freedom brings with it responsibility and consequences.

- Continuing to gather information about the uniqueness of the college experience and the demands presented along with ideas of how others have successfully navigated these challenges will go a long way in reducing any concerns or distress experienced while contemplating the next phase of your life.

HOW DOES STRESS LOOK ON ME?

So the dentist has me buying some kind of mouth guard for when I sleep. Apparently, she thinks I am under stress since I'm grinding my teeth at night.

Well, grinding your teeth at night could be a signal that you are under stress, but it is neither a common signal nor is it the only signal. According to the American Institute of Stress (yes ... there really is an institute of stress, check it out at http://www.stress.org/self-assessment/), stress comes in a variety of shapes, sizes, and impacts.

Because of the highly unique way stress can be experienced by each of us, as well as the different effects in can have on our health and well-being, it is worthwhile to step back in order to understand what stress looks like and feels like on you. It is also important that you (and we) increase your sensitivity and awareness of those moments when you are stressed. This awareness is essential as the first step to managing your stress.

4.1: Shouldn't It Be Obvious?

Shouldn't it be obvious that a person should know when he is dealing with a level of stress that is unhealthy? The answer is not so simple.

First of all, stress comes in a variety of shapes and sizes and its impact can vary from the very obvious to the less-than-easy to detect. In addition, the way stress shows up on your friends and family (teeth grinding?) may not be the same way it shows on you. There is quite a variation in our stress response, both in form and intensity.

Another problem with knowing when we are stressed is that many of the effects of stress can look like other forms of illness or physical disruption and thus be misdiagnosed. That upset stomach you feel or even the repetitive cold you catch can be easily attributed to a late night pizza with a nose-running, sniffling, coughing "friend." But perhaps the most insidious and subtle reasons we fail to recognize our stress and its impact is that we are simply ... get ready ... *simply used to it*!

Believe it or not, repeated stress can desensitize us to the experience of stress. We may even habituate to the point where we experience stress as our natural state, thus making it more difficult to recognize stress symptoms as detrimental. For example, have you ever been at school or work or some place where there is a noisy air conditioner? You spend time there and before long you don't even notice or hear the rattle. In fact, you may have actually gotten startled when this noisy air conditioner goes off and it is suddenly quiet. Yep, that is habituation! We simply get so used to something that it seems to be a natural part of our life or our current situation. And this desensitization, this habituation, can happen to our own reaction to our stress responses, be they grinding teeth, upset stomach, neck tension, or even headaches. And while you may find it hard to believe that such body conditions can simply be "not-experienced," consider the example of an individual who has a heart condition such as atrial fibrillation where his pulse or heart rate may become erratic and begin to race. It is not all that unusual for those individuals to become so used to the condition that they don't even notice that they are in AFib until they step onto a treadmill and see that the monitor is going nuts. Or consider the awakening that one student got when he encountered "relaxation" as an unusual state (see Voices From Campus 4.1) or as he states, "Relaxing stresses me out!"

VOICES FROM CAMPUS 4.1

Renaldo—Relaxation as Stressful!

Background: Renaldo is a junior, physics major at an Ivy League school. He is quite active on campus, being on a soccer scholarship, serving as elected Junior Class representative, and chairing the rush committee for his frat. To say Renaldo is busy would be an understatement. Well as it happened he signed up for a psychology "wellness" course this semester as an elective. As part of the course the teacher worked the class through a meditation/progressive relaxation program. It was during the third session of this program that Renaldo almost freaked out.

Voices:

So we are in the process of a deep-breathing exercise and working on mindfulness. The room was dark, we are all on our mats, eyes closed and there were background sounds of wind and ocean waves. As I continued to breathe slowly and rhythmically and tried to clear my mind focusing on the moment, I suddenly jumped as if electrified. It wasn't painful, just weird. It was something like I have experienced when I was falling asleep and would kind of jump but different. I mean it really freaked me out. The class looked at me like they thought I had been electrified or something, and the professor came over to see if I was okay.

As she spoke with me I realized that what I was freaking out about was that I was relaxing. I mean my breathing was really calm and my body felt warm and all my muscles were super relaxed. I can't ever remember feeling like that. When I think of it now, it was really cool, really enjoyable. But for some reason it freaked me out. My professor suggested that the state of relaxation was such a contrast to my normal rapid breathing, tense body posture that it may have set off a mental alarm.

Wow, talk about weird. Relaxing stresses me out! (laughs).

Certainly being desensitized to being in an ongoing state of stress is not good, in fact it can be life threatening. Clearly if stress becomes our "norm" we will not take the steps needed to reduce it; thus the cumulative long-term negative effects will have a fertile ground to develop.

4.2: Scales ... Scales ... Scales

Given the possibility that we may not even be aware of our stress and the damage it is doing, it would appear that the very first step to stress management is for us to increase our awareness of stress in our life and the degree to which we are affected by stress. There are numerous scales, questionnaires, and online services that have been developed to assist in the assessment of one's experience of stress.

Some of these questionnaires have been around for quite a while and they measure the number of major stressors we may be encountering. For example, one measure which you might have seen is the Holmes-Rahe Life Stress Inventory. This scale assesses the impact of major life change events, things like the death of a close family member, getting married, pregnancy, or even changing to a different line of work. The scale assigns points to each of some 43 life change events and then asks you to total your score. For those with 150 or less, the authors suggest a low risk to stress-induced health problems. However for someone who scores 300 or more points, they suggest an 80 percent chance of experiencing stress-induced health problems. Wow!

While this scale measures major life change events, there are other scales that rate those day-to-day minor annoyances, things ranging from losing your keys or being stuck in a traffic jam to some of the negative verbal encounters we all experience every day (you know the person at Starbucks?). One of the scales that measures these types of daily stressors is appropriately named the *Hassles and Uplifts Scales* (HSUP), created by Richard Lazarus and Susan Folkman (1999). If interested, you can access that scale and have a computer-generated report provided for approximately $15. It is available at http://www.mindgarden.com/108-hassles-uplifts. If you go to their website, you will be given a login that you can use to take the survey and monitor your progress, with reports generated as you wish.

But perhaps one of the scales that most directly addresses your current "state of life" was that created by Kohn, Lafreniere and Gurevich (1990). It is called *The Inventory of College Students' Recent Life Experiences* (ICSRLE).

This, of all the scales, may prove most useful to you as you begin to transition into college life.

The ICSRLE was designed to identify individual exposure to sources of stress or hassles encountered by college students. Now, while you may not have entered campus or perhaps just started and are therefore not aware of all that you will encounter, it still may be useful to take a look at the scale and the sources of stress one may encounter as a college student (see Your Turn 4.1). This review could prove helpful in your own preparation for dealing with life as a college student.

YOUR TURN 4.1

The Inventory of College Students' Recent Life Experiences

The following inventory can be helpful in assessing personal exposure to these sources of stress or hassles. This inventory also allows for an identification of the extent to which those stressors are experienced over the past month.

Directions: Please indicate for each experience how much it has been a part of your life over the past month. Mark your answers according to the following guide:

Intensity of Experience Over the Past Month

0 = not at all part of my life
1 = only slightly part of my life
2 = distinctly part of my life
3 = very much part of my life

_____1. Conflicts with boyfriend's/girlfriend's/spouse's family
_____2. Being let down or disappointed by friends
_____3. Conflict with professor(s)
_____4. Social rejection
_____5. Too many things to do at once
_____6. Being taken for granted
_____7. Financial conflicts with family members
_____8. Having your trust betrayed by a friend
_____9. Separation from people you care about

Paul M. Kohn, Kathryn Lafreniere, and Maria Gurevich, "The Inventory of College Students' Recent Life Experiences: A Decontaminated Hassles Scale for a Special Population," *Journal of Behavioral Medicine*, vol. 13, no. 6. Copyright © 1990 by Springer Publishing Company. Reprinted with permission.

_____10. Having your contributions overlooked
_____11. Struggling to meet your own academic standards
_____12. Being taken advantage of
_____13. Not enough leisure time
_____14. Struggling to meet the academic standards of others
_____15. A lot of responsibilities
_____16. Dissatisfaction with school
_____17. Decisions about intimate relationship(s)
_____18. Not enough time to meet your obligations
_____19. Dissatisfaction with your mathematical ability
_____20. Important decisions about your future career
_____21. Financial burdens
_____22. Dissatisfaction with your reading ability
_____23. Important decisions about your education
_____24. Loneliness
_____25. Lower grades than you hoped for
_____26. Conflict with teaching assistant(s)
_____27. Not enough time for sleep
_____28. Conflicts with your family
_____29. Heavy demands from extracurricular activities
_____30. Finding courses too demanding
_____31. Conflicts with friends
_____32. Hard effort to get ahead
_____33. Poor health of a friend
_____34. Disliking your studies
_____35. Getting "ripped off" or cheated in the purchase of services
_____36. Social conflicts over smoking
_____37. Difficulties with transportation
_____38. Disliking fellow student(s)
_____39. Conflicts with boyfriend/girlfriend/spouse
_____40. Dissatisfaction with your ability at written expression
_____41. Interruptions of your schoolwork
_____42. Social isolation
_____43. Long waits to get service (e.g., at banks, stores, etc.)
_____44. Being ignored
_____45. Dissatisfaction with your physical appearance
_____46. Finding course(s) uninteresting

_____47. Gossip concerning someone you care about

_____48. Failing to get expected job

_____49. Dissatisfaction with your athletic skills

Scoring the ICSRLE

Add your total points: _____

Your score on the ICSRLE can range from 0 to 147. Higher scores indicate higher levels of exposure to hassles. Focus on two key outcomes from your results. First, you can determine your current level of stress by adding your score for each hassle and getting a total. Second, you can discover which of the hassles play a greater part in your life. Higher scored items that you rated with a 3 indicate those stressors are more of an issue for you.

Whether facing the major challenges encountered throughout life or those unique to college life, the truth is that it is impossible to navigate through the day without being confronted by stressors. And while it is helpful to become aware of the barrage of demands we may be facing, as well as their potential impact on our well-being, you know from reading Chapter 2 that the major contributor to our stress response is our attitude and not the conditions in which we find ourselves. With this in mind, we invite you to take a look at the Perceived Stress Scale (see Your Turn 4.2). Unlike the other scales we mentioned, this scale assesses the effects of stress and can be much more helpful to our self-assessment and identification of our stress levels.

YOUR TURN 4.2

Perceived Stress Scale

Directions: The questions in this scale ask about your feelings and thoughts during the last month. In each case, you will be asked to indicate how often you felt or thought a certain way. Although some of the questions are similar, there are differences between them and you should treat each one as a separate question. The best approach is to answer fairly quickly. That is, don't try to count up the number of times you felt a particular way; rather indicate the alternative that seems like a reasonable estimate.

Sheldon Cohen, Tom Kamarck, and Robin Mermelstein, "Perceived Stress Scale from A Global Measure of Perceived Stress," _Journal of Health and Social Behavior_, vol. 24, no. 4. Copyright © 1983 by American Sociological Association. Reprinted with permission.

For each question choose from the following alternatives:
0 – never 1, – almost never, 2 – sometimes,
3 – fairly often, 4 – very often

1. _____ In the last month, how often have you been upset because of something that happened unexpectedly?

2. _____In the last month, how often have you felt that you were unable to control the important things in your life?

3. _____In the last month, how often have you felt nervous and stressed?

4. _____In the last month, how often have you felt confident about your ability to handle your personal problems?

5. _____In the last month, how often have you felt that things were going your way?

6. _____In the last month, how often have you found that you could not cope with all the things that you had to do?

7. _____In the last month, how often have you been able to control irritations in your life?

8. _____In the last month, how often have you felt that you were on top of things?

9. _____In the last month, how often have you been angered because of things that happened that were outside of your control?

10. _____In the last month, how often have you felt difficulties were piling up so high that you could not overcome them?

Your PSS Score

You can determine your PSS score by following these directions:
First, reverse your scores for questions 4, 5, 7, and 8. On these four questions, change the scores like this: 0 = 4, 1 = 3, 2 = 2, 3 = 1, and 4 = 0.
Now add up your scores for each item to get a total. **My total score is _____.**
Individual scores on the PSS can range from 0 to 40, with higher scores indicating higher perceived stress.

Interpreting Your Score

Scores ranging from 0–13 would be considered low perceived stress.
Scores ranging from 14–26 would be considered moderate perceived stress.
Scores ranging from 27–40 would be considered high perceived stress.

4.3: Increasing Personal Awareness—Being Mindful

As should be obvious, there are more than enough scales, websites, and self-directed assessment tools available to assess the state of your life (in terms of stressors) and your reactions to those demands. But carrying around scales and assessment tools is certainly not practical, and waiting for printed results to return from some assessment company doesn't appear very useful in the moment.

Clearly, if you are to attack stress in the moment, you will need to be aware that you are stressed *in* the moment. So perhaps the best tool for knowing that you are stressed is knowing how stress "looks on you" or is experienced by you.

So let's begin to pay attention.

Pay attention and increase your awareness and mindfulness about your bodily reactions are when you are stressed. Being sensitive to the appearance of these reactions will allow you to employ them as major warning signals or indicators that you are in the grips of stress and something needs to be done.

Your Turn 4.3 invites you to reflect on your experience with a number of bodily symptoms. As you review the list, consider those that appear to be good indicators of your experience under stress. Becoming aware of these and monitoring their appearance can serve as your own personal stress alarm and remind you to a step back, or step out, and engage in strategies to manage your stress, strategies that we will discuss in the upcoming chapters.

YOUR TURN 4.3

Monitoring My Stress Response

Directions: The following "symptoms" have been associated with a number of conditions, including stress. Identify those symptoms that you encounter frequently and see if you can find a link, an association, to times of stress-demands. You may find that your heightened awareness of the presence of these symptoms at any one time can help you take the steps needed to manage that stress.

Symptoms / Experience	Frequency of These Symptoms						
	Almost All Day/ Every Day	Couple of Times a Day	Once Daily	Couple of Times a Week	Once a Week	Once a Month	Never
headache							
difficulty sleeping							
stomach upset / nausea							
diarrhea or cramps							
difficulty falling asleep							
difficulty staying asleep							
fatigue							
heart racing / palpitation							
chest pain							
excessive sweating							
cold or sweaty hands or feet							

dry mouth / difficulty swallowing							
clenched jaw or grinding teeth							
knots in your shoulders, a stiff neck, or your lower back cramped up							

4.4: The Take Away

- Life stressors—big ones and minor hassles—barrage us all.

- While perhaps we can assess the number and intensity of life stressors, it is more important to be aware of our reaction to these stressors and the impact they may have at the moment and for the long run.

- There are numerous measures that you can use to assess your current state of stress.

- Knowing how to identify when you are stressed is not always easy, especially if you are becoming accustomed to it.

- Increasing your awareness of those body changes and experiences that signal you are stressed—be it a stiff neck, or headache, or jaw clenching and teeth grinding—is the first step to learning to manage that stress.

UNIT II: DEMANDS . . . DEMANDS . . . AND MORE DEMANDS

COLLEGE—A DIFFERENT WORLD!

I'm here! I made it! Little nervous, but hey it's me calling the shots now. Take the courses I like, eat what I want, hang with whomever I choose, basically do what I want, when I want. Yep ... I made it.

It may sound like a dream come true—your own routine for eating, sleeping, studying, maybe some partying. Nobody on your case to clean your room, do your homework, eat breakfast. You can do whatever! What can be stressful about that?!

As you have read in previous chapters, stress comes from stressors. How you react to these stressors can create a productive outcome or may cause deterioration of your health and well-being. So how could anything but happiness come out of this newfound independence and "new world"?

College is not just about going to class, completing homework, and doing some extracurricular activity such as a sport or club. College is totally different, and with change comes the opportunity for stress to not only surface but also take over. It is something that can really sneak up on you. Just consider the experience of one freshman that found life going from nirvana to just shy of Dante's inferno (see Voices From Campus 5.1).

VOICES FROM CAMPUS 5.1

College Life is Easy! Oh, Not Really!

Wow, I thought this was unbelievable! The first month of my freshman year was fantastic! I met so many new people and made so many friends. I played my music whenever I wanted and spent hours talking to people all night. Classes didn't seem bad, and they only met a couple times a week. If I was tired, I could skip a class or two and it didn't matter. I felt like I had so much free time and I loved it! I never had to really study to get good grades, so I was sure I'd do fine on my tests, and there were only around three tests in each class. This was going to be easy. It was great to be away from home where there was someone watching what I was doing. I was fine on my own.

Then came the first round of tests in my classes. What?! Talk about a wake-up call. I mean, what were all those questions that I had no idea about? You mean I really had to read all those hundreds of pages in the text?! When was I supposed to do that? I couldn't believe I did so horribly because I was a great student! I had a great social life going, but my parents were not going to be happy!

As you can imagine, this freshman had no idea about college in all of its glory and demands and as such was clearly caught off guard, much to the detriment of her GPA! It is really helpful to step back and try to get a more realistic picture of the opportunities and challenges you are about to face. What do you think will be different between your high school and your college experiences? A list has been started for you to consider these differences as you look at Your Turn 5.1.

YOUR TURN 5.1

College is Definitely Not High School!

Directions: Clearly the high school experience is different than what you will encounter in college. While everyone will experience the degree of difference and the challenges it may present in their own way, it is important to at least try to anticipate these differences so that you may be better able to turn the challenge into something to be enjoyed. Below is a chart with some areas of contrast for your considerations. Add to the list as you wish, and for a more detailed list see *How Is College Different from High School* (Southern Methodist University) http://www.smu.edu/Provost/ALEC/NeatStuffforNewStudents/HowIsCollegeDifferentfromHighSchool.

High School	College
Teachers take attendance and may make sure you receive missed assignments	Professors may not know if you are in class, and you are typically responsible for getting any missed work
Assignments have short-term due dates	You may have to set your own schedule to complete assignments
Your course selection and graduation requirements are fairly specific	Your course selection and graduate requirements are your responsibility
You may have to study a few days before a test	You may be responsible for an entire semester of information and may need to study many hours and days each week
Your routine is structured	
You have a curfew	

As you can see, there may be many differences between high school and college. When expectations are not clear, or not understood, pressure starts to build. Then (Boom!), before you know it, you are under the thumb of stress. But it is not just the failure to understand and prepare for the different demands and experiences you will encounter in college that serves as a source of stress. It starts from day one of the application process, but then you knew that. The Princeton Review's 2016 "College Hopes & Worries Survey," for example, reported the highest levels of stress were attributed to angst students felt even considering applications for college entrance. So if you are still in the midst of waiting for acceptance letters and feeling stress, you are not alone!

What else could cause stress? According to that same Princeton survey, the biggest worry and source of stress centered on the issues of finance. You think worrying about paying for gas, or prom, or senior week was stressful—just think about the cost of four years at the college of your choice. Wow, how will you pay for this debt?! Well, perhaps there are scholarships available. But even though scholarships help reduce the stress of financial concern, they introduce a new stress—that of concern about performance. What about grades to keep that scholarship? And then there is ...

Whoa!!!! Yes there are a number of real issues, real challenges that have to be addressed. Each will demand adaptation and thus, by definition, stress. But didn't we learn something about how we react to stressors and how it can color the impact stress has on us? Remember? We can minimize the stress to the point that we simply ignore the demand, which will only come back to bite us, or we can blow it way out of proportion and most likely blow our fuse. With this kind of reaction we can take what was a real problem, even a big one, and make it unreasonably huge and unmanageable. It can become a real threat to our mental well-being.

A study by the Center for Collegiate Mental Health noted that in 2016 anxiety and depression were the most commonly reported concerns of college students, and it was a trend that appeared to be on the rise. While the later chapters of this book will provide you with the tools to manage your stress and avoid such emotional upset, the one thing that you could do right now is move away from the approach of ignoring stressors or exaggerating them to trying to get a handle on the real nature of the problems and demands you are about to encounter. Such a realistic view will help you maintain a balanced perspective on the stress and, with it, the ability to engage in productive problem solving. So for now, let's try to understand what else may cause stress so we can know what to expect. You may want to consider making a short-term and a long-term goal for each of these sections after you have read through them.

5.1: Academics

Your courses and the challenges you encounter engaging with them will most certainly be different than what you experienced in high school. You will be expected to take more responsibility for your own learning. You will not only be required to comprehend the material but more likely to go to higher levels of thinking in order to analyze and apply what you have learned. And the material itself won't be confined to a handout or a chapter or even a PowerPoint presentation. Often you will need to go beyond these materials to review research or alternative sources so that you more clearly grasp what is taught. Sounds exhausting! It can be, but that is all it should be—exhausting, not devastating. Remember this isn't about three credits or a grade, your courses are helping to form you and prepare you for a lifelong career. And the need to be your own best teacher and advocate doesn't stop with the complexity and expansiveness of the material.

Remember those high school classes of about 25 to 30 students? Depending on your coursework and the size of your college, you may be sitting in some classes with several hundred students. The professor may not always know you are there, so it may be up to you to decide if you want to get the most of your college experience by attending class and putting forth your best effort. Thinking you can just get "lost" in those large classes? Yep, you could! But at what cost? At what cost to your future and at what expense of missed opportunity?

This is a time for you to take the initiative. It's your life and your future, so take charge. Build your network. Get to know people. Connect with other students for a study group or to compare notes. Wait … notes? Yes, notes. Not everything to be learned is in your book. Professors love to pontificate regarding their field of study, so it helps to listen and take notes. If you are like one the authors of this book and find that you frequently take mental vacations during lectures, ask your professor if you can record the lecture. This will pay off when studying for those tests or writing papers.

For many of your courses you may only have a few tests or papers per class for the semester, so make them count! Also use the campus resources to help you with your assignments and tests. For example, most campuses have writing centers and tutoring services available for help with papers and projects. Take advantage and use these resources, you're paying for it! Finally, if you haven't already, get to know your learning style and use that knowledge to your advantage. Are you a person who truly concentrates better with background noise or do you need absolute silence? Do you seem to focus better when in an informal environment or does a library or study desk work better for you? Consider some of the questions and links found in Your Turn 5.2. It is helpful to "study-up" on your preparedness to study!

YOUR TURN 5.2

Making Studying Meaningful

Being prepared is one way to alleviate stress, so being prepared for a test may decrease stress and increase performance!

Meaningful Studying

1. Do you know your preferred learning style? Find out a bit more at educationplanner.org (http://www.educationplanner.org/students/self-assessments/learning-styles.shtml).

2. Do you have the resources you need?

   Environment (space, noise level)

   Materials (books, papers, computer)

   Time (schedule, planner)

   Other

Find out more at academictips.org (http://www.academictips.org/acad/literature/notetaking.html) and testtakingtips.com (http://www.testtaking-tips.com/study/).

Although studying and academics are very important in college, and clearly need to be a top priority, there are plenty of other areas of college that impact your experience in college and your stress levels.

5.2: Social Life—Anyone?

Social life—yep, now we are talking! But maybe we should take a step back and remember that while this is important, actually very important, for your healthy development, we have to find a balance while addressing the academic demands. As you begin to increase your awareness of the demands encountered with meeting your academic requirements, you may also realize that you may need to decrease or take a break from extracurricular activities in order to concentrate on your studies. This doesn't mean, nor should it mean, giving up a social life and becoming an academic hermit. That's not healthy and actually it is counterproductive for your learning and your development. So even when reducing your previous social activities, you need to look for other opportunities to connect and to enrich your college journey with something aside from academics. No matter what your social life looks like, balancing it with your academic life will help keep stress at bay.

On a very practical level, expanding your social contacts and network may be a valuable resource for future employment. Many alumni, whether they were fraternity brothers, sorority sisters, or team members find themselves in positions of hiring—so having a previous connection can pay dividends. But even without such a "career" focus and value, your social life is important to your healthy development. Connecting with other people helps us to feel like we belong and can enhance our emotional well-being. Finding activities, clubs, services we enjoy can lead to greater health and well-being, and it can lead to your development as a "whole person" not just an academic. The formational value of the out-of-classroom engagement is clearly seen in Voices From Campus 5.2.

VOICES FROM CAMPUS 5.2

To Join or Not to Join?!

When I first started college I was hesitant to join any clubs or organizations. I didn't want anything to interfere with my studying and GPA. I watched my roommate join everything, and he pledged a fraternity his first semester. That was crazy! He never had time to do his classwork or study for tests. He wound up on probation and he was dropped from his major. I just went to class and studied.

By the time spring semester started, I had a decent GPA, but I felt like all I did was go to the library. The second week of the semester, one of the kids in my communications class asked if I was going to help out at the Human Resource Fair the following week. I hadn't thought about going, but why not? I was so glad I went! I didn't really like helping, but I learned about a communications club that sounded like it had events that were just like what I wanted to do after I graduated.

Even better, I met a professor I hadn't had for class yet who needed help with a college-wide project that sounded so cool, and he asked me to work on the project with him! This was great experience and will be great for my résumé!

For more ideas of the types of extracurricular opportunities that may be available at college, check out this website: http://education.stateuniversity.com/pages/1855/College-Extracurricular-Activities.html. As you review these various opportunities try to identify your own short-term and long-term goals in regards to your collegiate social life, and consider which of these may best serve you in achieving those goals.

So a social life is or can be valuable to your collegiate development. You may have noticed we said "can be." The caveat is that you need to remember the balance of social and academic. Without a structured routine for studying, extracurricular activities and social engagements can pull you into an academic slump. Probably the clearest challenge comes in the form of … parties. Yes, parties are great ways to gather with like-minded peers and let off some steam, or celebrate big wins, end-of-semester finals, and the sun coming up. But like most things, moderation and balance are essential if you are to grow through these experiences. You know, but we will tell you anyway … too much party time and perhaps too much alcohol time can result in not just decreased grades, but decreased health, well-being, or worse. So while the ad invites you to "do it," we invite you to do it with an eye toward a healthy balance.

5.3: Daily Life: Surviving Life as a College Student

Hey, you made it this far, so okay, maybe you now have to think about juggling classes, homework, extracurricular activities, getting involved but not overly involved, caring for yourself (where's Mom when you need her), watching the weight (all those desserts, yikes), registering for the next semester, and so many other things. This is a lot to think about! And as you move through the remaining chapters we will help you develop the insights and skills you need to navigate and survive daily life as a college student, starting right now.

One of the ways you can easily add to your productivity and happiness, starting right now, is by keeping self-care in the forefront of your thoughts. It may seem too easy, but taking care of your basic needs such as food, sleep, and time to reflect will go a long way to help you adjust, adapt, and cope with the stress of new demands. And while caring for your body is an essential element, caring for you spirit is just as essential. So take a breath. Seriously. Caring for yourself can start with taking time out of your fast-paced, stress-filled world to focus on the joy and gift of being you at this moment. Take a breath. Slow yourself, your world for a moment each day, starting now.

As you begin to develop your stress response tool kit think about including the practice of mindfulness; the following link is a great place to start: http://www.mindful.org/meditation/mindfulness-getting-started/.

5.4: The Take Away

- College is different than high school! Think about these differences ahead of time and be prepared.
- Set goals for your academic life, social life, and daily survival.
- Be assertive by asking questions and taking initiative.
- Take control (of your time, your plan, your way).
- Find and practice balance in your life.
- Take a breath—keep perspective. Things are as they are, no worse, no better just challenges that you have the ability to face.

BEING FREE TO BE: THE CHALLENGE OF INCREASED AUTONOMY

So I can do this. I can take care of myself and prove
I can be independent. I … I … hope I can.

Being at college, especially if you are living away from home, gives you the opportunity to exercise your independence and truly make many decisions on your own. These decisions can range from how you want to spend your "free time" or what and when to eat, up to more important things like whether or not you go to class or if and when to do your homework. This freedom is exciting and can feel very empowering. But increased autonomy brings increased responsibility, and with increased responsibility comes the possibility of increased stress. This experience of freedom and independence can be overwhelming and very stressful, especially if you fail to engage good planning and decision making. Just consider the wake-up call received by one freshman, Silvia (see Voices From Campus 6.1).

VOICES FROM CAMPUS 6.1

Decisions Gone Bad

Silvia was a top student in her high school and was so excited to get into college as a first-generation student. Her parents were very strict and she had made them proud with her academic accomplishments and exemplary behavior. She had never caused them concern as she only dated bright young men from the same ethnic background, always made it home by her 11:00 p.m. curfew, and had never tried smoking or alcohol. Until now, Silvia had relied on her parents to help with all her decisions.

Her first night on campus, Silvia quickly discovered all the rules she followed at home had nothing to do with what all the other students were doing. Her 11:00 p.m. curfew was the same time everyone in the dorm started their evening festivities. Well, she needed to make friends, right? Off she went and, like her peers, stayed out until the wee hours of the morning and did quite a bit of partying. She slept through her first class. When she woke up, she didn't know what to do. She wasn't used to making her own decisions. For that matter, she wasn't used to doing anything for herself. As she put her head back down on the pillow, she wondered if it mattered that she missed class, and how she was going to get her laundry done, and what should she wear when she went out later that night …

A few weeks later Silvia's parents came to campus for Family Day. They were shocked to find that their formally well-put-together daughter had lost 10 pounds and was wearing scraggly, dirty clothes. When confronted, Silvia admitted to her parents that she had missed some classes and hadn't figured out how to do her laundry. They told her she obviously wasn't ready to live at college and to pack her things—she was going home.

As you read, Silvia was not prepared for her newfound independence. The fact that she did not experience a lot of independence and autonomy prior to coming to college resulted in her inability to make appropriate choices at college. Having experience with making your own decisions is certainly helpful. As such, it may be useful to take a snapshot of your own experience with autonomy (see Your Turn 6.1).

YOUR TURN 6.1

Making an Informed Decision

Directions: There are many decisions that you must make every day. Look at the following list of typical tasks that are to be completed each day and reflect on who is responsible for when it is completed when you are in high school and who is responsible when you are in college. When you are finished, circle any tasks for which you would like more information, and then connect with someone who will enlighten you!

Daily tasks	Who does/decides while in high school?	Who does/decides while in college?	Do I need more information?
Ex. Dinner (what time and what to eat?)	Parent	Me	No
Ex. Laundry	Parent	Me	Yes
Homework/studying			
Getting to class			
Registering for courses, financial aid deadlines, etc.			
Breakfast and lunch			
Getting snacks			
Signing up or getting to events and extracurricular activities			
Other?			

In addition to having previous experience with making your own life decisions, it is also helpful to have a sense about the types of choices and decisions you will need to make, prior to actually experiencing them. Let's take a look at a number of the more typical responsibilities you will be juggling.

6.1: I Have to Manage What?!

You've already started working on your juggling when you applied to college, so what's next for you to manage? Aside from the daily routine of eating, sleeping, going to class, and studying, oh yeah, throw in some time for a social life and basically taking care of yourself, the following are tasks you may have to handle:

- Pay enrollment fee
- Apply for financial aid
- Find scholarships
- Apply for housing
- Get your campus ID card
- Watch for advising and registration activities
- Purchase your parking permit
- Submit immunization documentation
- Explore payment options
- Commuter resources
- Find a job
- Decide on your major or degree (tap into resources for career exploration)
- Find out how to get involved
- Make arrangements for any accommodations you are eligible for with student support services and then speak to professors about these accommodations
- Know and understand the student Code of Conduct—become familiar with the student handbook, academic honesty policy, and your rights and responsibilities as a student
- Check out the Academic Integrity policy
- Meet regularly with your academic advisor (once per semester)

Ouch, we know. Stop it, right? Well it does help to have an idea of what you are about to experience, so it may help to see a more complete list at https://www.kent.edu/artscollege/student-responsibilities-college. We also suggest that you explore the website and information for the specific college you will be attending.

6.2: It Feels Like a Lot— Not Sure You Can Do It?

So you have an idea, or maybe even know exactly where you will be going to college. But how about your major? Or even, how about what you want to do with the rest of your life? Talk about stress!

Actually, if you want to talk about maximum stress, let's assume that you not only have to know the answers to these questions right now but that once decided you don't get a second chance. If you are viewing the decisions you make today as forcing you down a path with no way off, it truly will be stressful.

If you are questioning your ability to handle life on your own and your ability to make all those choices that will have an effect on your future, you are not alone. This is typical for this time of your life. In fact, some people say it's exactly what you are supposed to think and feel. Consider Marcus' thoughts in Voices From Campus 6.2.

VOICES FROM CAMPUS 6.2

Marcus

How am I supposed to really know what I want to do the rest of my life? I think I'm supposed to know so I can choose my major and not waste my time or money in college. It has to be a career that lets me make enough money so I can get married and buy a house within a few years. And I have to get a job as soon as I graduate, because there is no way I'm going back home. This is the start of my independence, and I'm not going backwards by going back home. I'm just not sure if I should be an engineer—they make good money, but I hate math. I'd really like to do something with art because I love it and I'm really good at it. But come on, how successful can I be as an artist? By the time I make any money as an artist, all my friends will be married, have families, and living the good life. I need to be independent and act like an adult, and that means a great job. But what should I major in?!

Perhaps you have had thoughts similar to Marcus? There is a natural desire and drive to be more independent, more autonomous. But elevating that desire to a "must" or somehow connecting your personal worth to being perceived as this independent adult can elevate the stress felt. Remember, how we think about a situation can make it a stressor, or not! Take a minute and reflect on some of the possible "shoulds" you may be pondering in Your Turn 6.2.

YOUR TURN 6.2

Should or Need?

Directions: Consider the following thoughts and reflect on whether they are "shoulds" (something you think you are supposed to do) or something you need to do.

Thought	"Shoulds" (S) or Needs (N)?	Need for College?	Need After College?
Finish college in four years			
Know my major freshman year			
Know my career path			
Get the perfect job after graduation			
Buy a house			
Get married			
Explore career options			
Earn a high salary			
Other			

6.3: A Path of Emerging Adulthood

Rather than demanding that you have it all together, it may be much more effective to accept that perhaps it is very reasonable to be somewhat uncertain and question your future during this time of your life. Maybe it is more realistic and certainly more functional for you to accept that this is a journey and you have yet to arrive at your destination. Truly you are on the path toward adulthood and are in emerging adulthood.

If we define "adulthood" as a stage of development which is characterized by 1) the ability to be responsible for our own actions; 2) the freedom to make independent decisions; and 3) financial independence, then you can appreciate that these do not come automatically as a result of age (I'm over 21) or circumstance (I just graduated from college).

As an emerging adult, you will experience increasing freedom and responsibility and, believe it or not, even financial independence. As discussed by researcher Jeffrey Arnett, this time of emerging adulthood is a time of possibilities, one of personal exploration and self-focus, and even times of feeling in-between. It is an exciting time. It is or can be a worrisome time. But most of all it is a time of exploring, a time of emerging into the adult you will become. We encourage you to read more about these features at http://jeffreyarnett.com/articles.htm and in *Emerging Adulthood: The Winding Road From the Late Teens Through the Twenties* by J. Arnett. Understanding the gift, the challenge, and the shared experience of those transitioning to adulthood will not only give you a new perspective on autonomy, but will help normalize the various experiences you may encounter. And these, in turn, will be helpful in decreasing stress!

After reading about what you think being autonomous in college means, we invite you to create a few short—and long-term goals for yourself in Your Turn 6.3. Setting goals is a great strategy to help alleviate stress!

YOUR TURN 6.3

Creating Short- and Long-Term Goals

Directions: Reflect on the tasks and thoughts you considered in Your Turn 6.1 and 6.2. What are some of the needs you identified? Write a long-term goal for that need and then think of at least two short-term goals that will help you reach your long-term goal.

Need	Long-term Goal	Short—term Goals
Ex. Identify major	A satisfying and successful career	Take career inventories in high school or at the career center in college Talk to my advisor in my first semester
Ex. Self-care	Manage my daily life tasks	Learn how to do laundry Take a cooking lesson Research where the infirmary or health clinic is located

6.4: The Take Away

- There will be many new tasks that you will be responsible for when you are in college.
- It is helpful to look ahead and familiarize yourself with the policies and requirements of your institution.
- Look at the resources available to you to help with time management, course selection, assignments, and career exploration.
- Autonomy may look different than you think!
- No one expects you to have arrived ... you are EMERGING!
- Planning ahead will decrease stress!

ROOMMATES . . . DEADLINES . . . AND OTHER POTENTIAL ANNOYANCES

Wow—a roommate, is that good? Someone to talk to anytime I want … or maybe someone who won't stop talking? What if I can't stand the person?!

You were thinking the hard part of college was over—you got in! Okay, so you did realize you would probably have to work, and work hard in your classes. However, there are other things that come with attending college, and some of these can become really annoying if you let them, especially if you don't do something about them. Throughout the previous chapters you have read how stressors can wind up making your health and your life miserable. By reading ahead, and planning ahead, you can better prepare yourself for some of the factors that can be potential annoyances, and instead make your college experience more successful and happy!

7.1: Roommates

If you plan on living on campus, one of the first adjustments you may encounter is having a roommate. Some colleges invite you to share information as to your preferences for a housing mate, and in some circumstances you may get to choose your roommate. Regardless, when you live with someone there are many factors that can potentially become annoyances! (See Voices From Campus 7.1.)

VOICES FROM CAMPUS 7.1

Roommate or Cellmate?!

I thought it would be easier to room with someone I knew—not only knew, but someone who is a good friend! We have so much in common and always had a good time together, and having been on the same track team we had spent a lot of time together. Wow—I was totally wrong! Even before we got to the dorm his mother wanted us to get "coordinating comforters"—seriously?! I was pulling out a blanket from my closet for my bed. And then he wanted to hang pictures on the wall from an anatomy book because he was pre-med. He thought that if he saw pictures of the skeleton and heart it would motivate him. No way! The walls should be covered with posters of Jimi Hendrix and the Beatles.

But the absolute worst part was when we moved in because I found out—he is a SLOB!! Underwear and wet towels all over the place—I can't take that! And it doesn't bother him! I tried talking with him and letting him know the towels can get moldy and smelly, and nobody will want to hang out in our room—but he doesn't care! And he never leaves the room except for classes and to eat, so I never have any privacy. I don't understand him—I thought he was so cool. I can't imagine what he's thinking. Doesn't he want anyone coming to the room? Doesn't he like me as a roommate? I don't know if I'm going to make it through the semester having to live like this.

The issues may not be a difference in decorating the room or preferred style of music, but chances are there will be issues that can cause your relationship with your roommate and your living conditions to be strained and stress filled. Think about it—you are in a room with another person, or a few other people. In some cases, that room, that space, is the only place to sleep, work, think, or just be. A place for privacy, or just alone time, may not be easy to come by unless you say something to your roomie or don't mind going to the basement of the library on a regular basis! There may be many opportunities for compromise; however, you will have to share your needs and listen to the needs of your roommate. Your resident advisor may be helpful for situations you cannot settle; however, in Your Turn 7.1 we invite you to reflect on your daily living habits to identity your needs and where you are able to compromise.

YOUR TURN 7.1

Successful Living With a Roommate

Directions: Reflect on the tasks below to help identify what makes you comfortable in a living arrangement. Next, identity a way to modify the tasks or compromise if your roommate has a different need.

Task	Modification	Compromise
Listening to music to fall asleep	Turning the volume down as low as possible	Listening to white noise or a genre you both enjoy
Keeping the lights on late to read	Using a book light aimed at the book	Creating a schedule for some late nights and some earlier nights
Bringing visitors to the room	Setting up a "visiting" time	Always asking each other first before inviting a guest in
Early riser vs. sleeping late		
Eating food with strong odors in the room		
Other		

When thinking about the process of compromising or, if you will, resolving conflict, it may be helpful to practice some of the principles suggested in the book *Getting to Yes* by Roger Fisher, William Ury, and Bruce Patton (2011). These authors suggest that successful negotiations can be aided if you:

1. **Separate the people from the problem.** Try not to make this a personal competition. In fact, try to understand the other person's position and needs.

2. **Focus on interests, not positions.** Remember the reason you want something to be a certain way is that it meets your needs. Focus on your goal. While you may have one idea on how to achieve those needs, there may be many paths that will lead to satisfaction. So don't get stuck arguing about one path … keep your eye on your interests, your goal.

3. **Learn to manage emotions.** It's important not to operate from your reptilian brain! This is not the end of the world. It is merely a problem, an inconvenience, a less-than-desirable state of affairs. So try to keep a rational perspective in "problem solving."

4. **Express appreciation.** Negotiation is hard. So remember to express appreciation for the willingness on the part of your roommate(s) to expend the time and energy to come to some mutually satisfying and perhaps creative way of meeting everyone's needs.

In short, the idea is to list what all parties are attempting to accomplish and to brainstorm and think creatively about the various ways that you all could go about accomplishing that. Your Turn 7.2 invites you to give it a try.

YOUR TURN 7.2

Getting to Yes

Directions: Below you will find a "typical" conflict that can emerge when settling in with a new roommate. Your task (one which may be aided by working with another) is to develop and select a creative pathway that would result in maximum satisfaction for all involved. Follow the steps below.

Conflict: Roommate likes to play music when studying late at night and you are a person who needs or benefits from quiet.

Step 1: Is your roommate a jerk? Or is it possible that there are different learning styles, one in which background noise is useful and one where background noise is distracting? If yes, then can we separate the person from the problem???

Step 2: Below, identify at least two needs which each roommate is attempting to satisfy or meet. It may be helpful to see the use or disuse of the music as a strategy to achieving a goal rather than the goal itself. (See example in chart.)

Step 3: Given the identified needs, brainstorm at least five possible ways of satisfying all of the needs listed. Get creative—crazy—think out of the box (this is where another person may be helpful).

Step 4: Review your strategies and try to identify the costs (physical, financial, social, etc.) and benefits (again, physical, financial, social, etc.) for each strategy.

Step 5: Select the strategy that appears to provide the biggest benefit to cost!

Step	Focus	Illustration	Your Response
Step 1:	Separate person from interest: Are your roommate's interests/ needs legitimate?	We have different learning styles and she does better with background noise, whereas I do better in quieter study environments.	
Step 2:	Need Identification	Me: Get good grades Roommate: Get good grades	(identify two for each)
Step 3:	Brainstorm Strategies	Take turns studying in the room—with other person going to library (me) or student union (roommate)	(get creative ... list five)

| Step 4: | Cost/Benefit | Cost of strategy is being displaced, maybe we have a lot of material to transport, the weather may stink, we might like to study in pj's, etc. The benefits are that at least we would stop arguing and would each have some time to study in the room and at an alternative setting that should work. | (list all costs and benefits for all options) |
| Step 5: | Selection | Let's try strategy #4! (We know we didn't list a strategy 4 ... that's where you come in.) | (your choice) |

Before moving on from our thoughts about a roommate, it's nice to consider a few benefits of this relationship. Your roommate may be someone to hang out and go places with, possibly someone to help you study, and very importantly, your roommate can be invaluable when your forget your key! Yep, another potential annoyance can arise if you aren't organized and attentive and you forget things—like your key. Being as organized and prepared as possible will be very helpful for assignments, tests, deadlines, and getting into your room.

7.2: Deadlines

Whether you are prone to be forgetful or not, there are a lot of things you will be responsible for remembering, like deadlines. You may never have realized how many deadlines there are, and you may be amazed at how many there are for which you are responsible! Assignments, tests, course registration, financial aid forms, scholarship applications, dorm or room assignments, advising appointments, whoa!!! There are more!! Stressed yet?! How will you know about these deadlines? Whew—take a breath . . . remember how good taking a nice, deep breath can be.

In the last chapter we talked about being autonomous and the responsibilities that may entail. Managing deadlines is one of those duties. We suggested finding out as much about college rules, policies, and events as possible ahead of starting the semester. Being prepared is one of the best ways to decrease or alleviate stress when it comes to deadlines, tests, and just getting through the day. With the convenience of the Internet, you can search through college and financial aid websites for many items that have deadlines. On campus, check with the resources available such as your resident advisor and academic advisor until you have an answer and are pointed in the right direction. Once you have dates and deadline details, find a way to organize the information in a format that works best for you. A calendar is a great tool, be it digital, electronic, paper, poster, or pocket size—whatever you will use on a regular basis. Make it a point to look ahead at least once a week to what is coming up and what you need to do. Take a few minutes to practice now making a list of your own deadlines in Your Turn 7.3.

YOUR TURN 7.3

To-Do List

Directions: Think about tasks that are pending now, when they are due, and what you need to do to accomplish the task. When you start the semester, listen during orientation and check with advisors for upcoming deadlines.

Task	Date Due	What do I have to do?
Send in deposit for college	May 1	Remind parents or write a check
Register for classes	June 15	Get online to register
Send in information for on-campus residency	June 30	Send back information via letter or email
Re-apply for financial aid	October 1	Fill out forms; get copy of last submittal
Other		

7.3: Other Potential Annoyances

For those of you who skipped over the roommate section because you will be commuting, consider one of the biggest potential annoyances that comes with living off campus: parking. Ugh!! If you don't take public transportation, parking can cause more stress than you might imagine having during finals week, and who wants to start their day with that?! Come early, get a spot, and get some work done! Consider the best time to arrive on campus when you are registering for next semester's classes. As you will read in Voices From Campus 7.2, many possible annoyances and causes of stress have to do with your classes.

VOICES FROM CAMPUS 7.2

Making Your Classes Count

Why am I in this class?! What does this biology class have to do with me being a social worker? I had biology in high school and I thought I was rid of it for good. I thought my classes would be interesting and what I wanted to study. I don't understand what these "gen ed" classes are and why I have to take them. I tried to drop it, but apparently I need it—I don't know what for! To make it worse, the class starts at 8:00 a.m. Do they really believe I can think about botany that early in the morning when I'm still struggling with getting out of the dorm in time? The class is in a big lecture hall with like 200 other tired freshmen. The professor talks on and on, and I can't even stay awake and pay attention.

And then there's the lab. The lab is from 1:00–4:00 p.m. on Friday—all Friday afternoon!! I don't like the class, I don't like the time, and I don't like the professor! I can't believe I'm paying money for this class. No wonder freshmen drop out!

There will be classes that you will be required to take to fulfill the requirements of your degree, and you may not like them all. The good news is that pretty much after your sophomore year, those classes and any prerequisite classes are completed and you will be in your major classes, the classes that will lead you into your career! In the meantime, the general education classes, or "gen eds," are meant to give you a solid foundation for your degree. So try to get the most out of them, and keep the stress at bay by getting to class on time and doing extra work for assignments and tests.

Challenges and potential annoyances such as class times and availability are a fact of life in college. Try flexible thinking and reframe your thoughts to "it's only 15 weeks" and maybe another class for my elective will work out okay. Hmm, about those elective classes. If you are lucky to be able to take an elective, think about making it something that will enrich your career or you as a person. Taking a course because your friend liked it doesn't always have the best outcome. You may not like the professor or the class! It may be helpful to put yourself in the professor's shoes—take her perspective and see if that changes your thinking. A professor who is teaching 200 tired freshmen has quite a challenge on her hands! Additional issues with classes, including not getting a required class or having a difficult time with a professor, will be situations that you should discuss with your advisor.

There may be several other potential annoyances you discover, such as being able to access resources, computer issues, and, of course, the quality and choice of FOOD! These are all issues that could increase your stress if not dealt with or handled by the appropriate people. Remember to communicate with your advisors, try flexible thinking, and prepare as much as possible. Being successfully autonomous means advocating for yourself, and in the case of potential annoyances, you have the choice to modify or change your expectations, let it go, or ask one of your resources for support. You can keep those potential annoyances from becoming real annoyances!

7.4: The Take Away

- College life includes many issues that if not planned for or dealt with could potentially become annoyances.
- It is helpful to communicate your needs with your advisors, professors, and roommate if you live on campus.
- If negotiating, remember to consider everyone's needs and creatively develop plans to maximize the satisfaction of all of those needs. This is not Win–Lose, but Win–Win.

- Using a calendar and lists of task will be helpful for meeting deadlines.

- Flexible thinking, or reframing your thoughts, will help put potential issues in perspective and provide alternative outcomes.

- You can make the choice to keep potential annoyances from becoming real annoyances by checking your resources, talking to advisors, and being willing to change your thinking!

UNIT III: STRESS-BUSTING TOOL BOX

IT STARTS IN YOUR HEAD

Men are disturbed not by things, but by the view which they take of them.

Epictetus

R eally, we get it. There is so much to do and there are so many things that you need to plan and prepare for, how could you NOT be stressed? Papers, interviews, and projects … the hits keep coming. But the wise, Greek-speaking, stoic philosopher Epictetus may have a slightly different view of your stress. His position, and that taken here, is that it's not the things of life that are stressful, but the way we take them!

The idea that external demands are the source of our stress is certainly intuitively appealing. However, as we noted in Chapter 2, research has demonstrated that the creation of distress versus eustress, and even the extent and duration of one's stress experience, is a result of one's *perspective* more than it is the result of the actual events encountered.

Okay, let's repeat that. It appears that the element most contributory to the nature of our stress experience is the perspective with which one approaches these experiences. It truly all starts in the mind!

Now, in order for us to not only understand this but also use this in order to gain power over our stress, we must reveal and attack the "big lie."

8.1: The Big Lie

One of the lies perpetuated by and in our society is that our emotions, including those identified as stress reactions, are created by external events. It's the "you made me mad" mindset. It seems as if the entire world shouts that you are NOT responsible for your emotional upset. If you have ever found yourself saying things like, "You really make me angry," "It's unfair, I never get a break," "This is horrible, I have too much to do," "I can't stand it!" then you have bought the lie.

8.2: The Truth

Most people will point to the events of life as the cause for their emotional reactions. They will point to things such as receiving a letter of rejection from a college admissions committee as the source of their depression or their desire to retreat to their rooms. It appears intuitively appealing to see the direct connection between an activating event and the consequences experienced. But upon further reflection and analysis it soon becomes apparent that it is NOT the activating event that directly causes the emotional and behavioral consequences, but rather it is the meaning or the interpretation one holds in regards to the event that is the sources of this emotional response. The letter is just a letter until we apply our personal meaning to it.

It is this personal meaning, this interpretation, this belief about this life event that can transform a simple letter into either a non-event, a minor disappointment, a problem to be solved, or a major disaster. It is the meaning we give to this letter that is the special ingredient resulting in our emotional and behavioral response.

We know this may be hard to swallow and you may be thinking, wait, if you get rejected it IS horrible. You may even be able to find a group of friends who would agree. They may all hold onto the idea that this rejection letter should be a cause of the depression, the crying, and the retreat to the room, after all, it is a disaster!

Well consider this. If the letter was truly the cause for the reaction, wouldn't all people receiving such a letter share that reaction? Think about it. Isn't it possible that some people might become angry, not sad or depressed? Maybe some experience relief believing that they don't have to move away from home or fearing that they would have failed. And there may even be some who see the rejection letter as disappointing, and perhaps something that motivates them to try harder. So how is it that the exact same activating event (getting rejected) can result in three different responses?

The answer? It is the person's belief about the meaning of the event, or the way each individual interpreted the activating event (receiving the letter), that gave form to the emotional consequences (e.g., depression, relief, inspiration, etc.). The external events are nothing more than experiences waiting to be INTERPRETED, and it is this interpretation that is causing the upset feelings in relationship to these less-than-desirable events. In order to make this point a bit clearer, we invite you to engage in Your Turn 8.1

YOUR TURN 8.1

Connecting Thoughts to Feelings

Directions: Consider the following situation and respond to the questions posed.

Situation:
So you just got your graduation gift. It is a brand-new Jeep Wrangler. You hop in, turn on your tunes, of course buckle up, and off the lot you go. What a rush!

As you sit waiting to merge into the oncoming traffic, you find yourself being smacked in the rear by this mammoth Cadillac Escalade. You can't believe the entire rear of your car is destroyed, somehow you were not even scratched, but the car ... HISTORY.

Task:

Below you will find thoughts that could have gone through your mind at the time of the accident. Write down how you would feel if you were in this situation and thinking this thought.

Thought	Emotional Reaction
Oh my god that was close—I could have died!!	
I can't believe that my brand-new car is totaled!	
Wow—I cannot believe my dad made me buy a special car insurance rider that pays me double if my car gets totaled.	
Wait, I know that guy, he's the fancy Cadillac/Porsche dealer.	
Thank goodness my mom is an accident lawyer.	

Reflection:

While the actual event was the same (your car totaled), did the emotional reactions vary as a result of the meaning you gave to that event? That is the connection of thought to feelings.

8.3: So?

Perhaps you are now saying; "Okay, that's interesting, but so what?" Well, here's the "so what." Understanding the power of our thinking can be very useful when attempting to manage stress.

While humans have the potential to be rational, reasonable, and functional beings, we also have the ability to misinterpret and even distort life events. Those distortions can create emotional and behavioral responses that are neither rational nor functional. Consider the case of Mr. Road Rage.

VOICES FROM CAMPUS 8.1

Mr. Road Rage

So I am trying to get across town to see my girlfriend and who is behind me? Reggie! He's all duded up. Check him out with his coat and tie. I know he is going for an internship interview. Well, as I turn onto Market Street, I have to slam the brakes. I am right in the middle of the homecoming parade.

I thought that wasn't going to be starting for another two hours. But here I am with floats and bands in front of me and a line of traffic blocking me. Well, so be it. But then I hear some honking and look back, it is Reggie. He beeps a few times and the next thing I know he is now laying on the horn. It's blasting. I'm looking in the mirror thinking, "like dude, mellow." But, no way, he now starts gunning the engine and is trying to go up on the sidewalk to get through the intersection. Look at him. He looks like he is going to stroke out. His face is red, he's cursing (thank goodness the windows are up) ... and oh, there is a motorcycle policeman now on his tail. Yep, he's stressed.

As we consider dear old Reggie in our illustration, a couple of things become very clear. First, we know he really wants to get to his internship interview. This is important to him, and in fact it is an important part of his education. But we also know that regardless of how important it is, his level of upset and his choices are neither helping him achieve that goal nor helping him reduce the stress of being stuck in traffic. In fact, we could argue that he is taking a disappointing situation and making it worse. Further, with the level of stress and apparent anger he is feeling, he is not even thinking clearly. Rather than going up on the sidewalk and thus incurring the wrath of a police officer, perhaps he should call the interviewer and explain that he will be late (and hopefully not in jail).

So why is he acting this way? Ask him and he will say it is because of this (expletive deleted) parade and traffic jam. Really? If that were true, then why aren't the other drivers stuck in the jam acting the same way?

It is very likely that among those stuck in the traffic jam there are others who have important places to be. But look at them. Some are out of their cars and sitting on the roof watching the parade, others look as if they are going to take a nap, and a few are on their cell phones. Only Reggie is sitting half on the sidewalk, now trying to avoid a heart attack while explaining his actions to the police officer.

So clearly a person is not automatically and maximally stressed by such a traffic jam. One becomes maximally stressed, like our dear Mr. Reggie, when he interprets these events as unbearable catastrophes! When we convince ourselves that one of life's inconveniences or problems is a major catastrophe, then we feel and act catastrophically.

Now what does that have to do with you?

8.4: Stress Reaction—Proportional to Actual Stressor?

As we noted in Chapter 2, stress is not something we can avoid, nor would we even want to avoid it. Stress is experienced anytime we are confronted with a situation that disrupts our equilibrium and requires us to make an adjustment, and that can be a source of personal growth.

So imagine that you look at your calendar and you realize that you have two tests coming up, as well as a major project and a classroom presentation. These are disruptors. These are stressors. These will require you to make a number of adjustments to your plans and your life, and your cognitive, physiological, emotional, and behavioral systems will all engage to make an adaptation to these demands. That's how it should work. It is also most likely how it does work, most of the time—when our experience of stress and our reactions to the stressors are proportional to the actual demands and required adjustments presented. As such, we continue to successfully navigate life.

But sometimes we distort the level of these demands. We sometimes misinterpret the nature of the situation and exaggerate the importance of the tasks and the potential danger. This certainly appears to be the case with Reggie, our Mr. Road Rage. And just like Reggie, if we interpret events as more dire, more catastrophic than they actually are, our reactions and stress experience will also be distorted and exaggerated since we are responding to what we believe to be true, rather than what is actually true.

Now we are not suggesting that as an adult you haven't faced issues in life that were potentially serious and quite challenging. But the truth remains that even when the events are serious, your thoughts about these events can make them worse than they are. An interesting illustration of this process can be found in the film *Titanic* which depicts the sinking of the luxury liner in the freezing waters of the North Atlantic. Now clearly for those on the ship who are most likely about to die, the level of stress is intense. In the film we see those on the sinking ship screaming, running about, jumping overboard, and generally trapped in a state of hysteria. Who could blame them? The ship is sinking and their lives are in danger. But it is not about blame. Our focus is on learning how to deal with reality in the best, least stressful manner possible.

So if we look at the facts of this situation along with the hysteria being demonstrated by those on the ship, the question to consider is this: Was such hysterical behavior an effective way to cope with the situation? Now perhaps you're thinking, "What's wrong with you? This panic, this hysteria is a normal reaction to such a catastrophic event!" And while it was certainly a common response for those depicted, we question whether it was the only response available and whether it was the best of responses. So if we return to a movie reference point, we see at least one other possible way of responding in the moments prior to the ship sinking. It is an alternative that appears to be much more effective in dealing with the actual stress encountered during this event than running around hysterically or jumping overboard into icy waters.

The scene to which we refer is one in which see a group of musicians standing on the deck of the sinking ship, instruments in hands, all beginning to play. These individuals chose to engage in an activity they loved. It was a process, that of making music, in which they found joy and perhaps comfort. Did it save their lives? NO. But as presented in the film, nothing would save their lives. So the choice they had during these moments before their impending death was to accept the reality that the ship would soon be underwater and that they would soon be dead. But here is the important point, at this moment they were still alive and they could respond with hysteria or with music. Their choice was to stay focused on the reality of the moment, rather than live in the moment of what will be. Thus, rather than becoming hysterical and, like so many others, spending the last moments of their lives in extreme anxiety and stress, they chose to take this moment of life and live it not in panic but in joy and love of the music they played.

Being able to stay focused on the facts, sticking to the reality of the demands, and refusing to catastrophize in the face of stress and life demands will require some work, much diligence, and a few simple steps!

8.5: Stay Grounded in Reality: See Things as They Are

The importance of staying grounded in reality when confronted with a significant stressor is illustrated in Voices From Campus 8.2.

VOICES FROM CAMPUS 8.2

Allison

Allison is a sophomore nursing student at a small Catholic college in her hometown. She did very well throughout her freshman year and generally excelled in her math and science courses. She came to the counseling office very upset, crying, and talking about dropping out. She described her reactions as follows:

"I have no idea how I am going to tell my parents. How do I face my friends? Everybody is counting on me. I am totally letting them down. Look at this paper (reaching for a research paper from her backpack)! There is more red ink on the page than there are printed words. I knew I couldn't do this. I am so ashamed of wasting my parents' money and getting their hopes up. I can't believe this (pointing to a grade of D+). I am not going to do anything stupid, like hurt myself, but I thought about it. This is the worst thing that ever happened to me and my family and I don't know what to do."

It is clear that Allison is truly upset and maximally stressed. The pain and the panic are real. But the basis upon which that reaction is founded appears less than a true reflection of reality and the challenges presented. Let's take a moment to consider the actual events of this situation. Do you have questions? How much does this grade contribute to the final grade? Will the professor allow a resubmission? What are her other grades in that class? Would failing this class result in her being kicked out of college? Clearly the only thing we know is that this paper was graded a D+. Without any other information, jumping to conclusions about failing out of school appears to be premature and outside the boundaries of what we know to be true. Further, when you review Allison's thinking it becomes clear that she has taken this D+ to reflect not just a score on her paper but evidence that she is a major disappointment to all who know her, especially her parents. Wow, that is a distortion of the facts, and Allison needs to be helped with gaining a more factual, evidential view of this event and the reality-based consequences that may result. As she does, her level of stress will be reduced proportionally and her reactions and responses will position her to better adapt and adjust to the challenge.

While you may not be as reactive and catastrophic as Allison, it is likely that you, like the authors, do look at all you have to do at any one time and at least momentarily believe that it is "all too much" or "impossible to do" or even "unfair." If you have ever had thoughts such as these, than you are distorting the actual task at hand and elevating your stress. After all, it is not too much nor impossible to do, nor even unfair, and it is most likely that you have experienced similar demands in the past and have successfully addressed them.

So when you feel stressed while waiting to hear about your college application, or trying to make sense out of a letter of rejection, or even attempting to organize and plan for all that you have to do in preparation for starting college, it is important to focus on "what is,"—nothing more and nothing less. It is important to identify the specific, factual demands that require your attention, then how you can adapt, and finally how you can control the tendency to exaggerate the level of threat or danger. It is important to learn how to "decatastrophize" when confronted by life's stressful events.

8.6: Decatastrophize: Become Aware of Your Thinking

Approach Life as a Scientist–Researcher

One useful way of gaining control over any tendency to distort and catastrophize is to approach those events that appear to be invitation to stress as a scientist–researcher might. As a scientist–researcher we would want to identify the specifics of the situation and the actual, reality-based consequences that most likely would result. Focusing on the specific data, the facts, the actual "what is," will help you avoid jumping to conclusions, especially conclusions that are catastrophic.

Write It Down and Debate With Yourself

A second strategy that helps keep us away from catastrophizing is to actually use paper and pencil to write down the specifics of the stressful demands. Writing it down versus simply working it out in your head introduces another mechanism that helps to prevent jumping to irrational, catastrophic conclusions.

Let's use the illustration with Allison. If you had a friend like Allison and you heard all the things she was saying, you would process her statements through all the additional facts you knew about her. You might know that her GPA was a 3.5 her freshman year. You might know that she has As in other courses. You might know her family loves her regardless. Or even if you didn't know these facts, you most likely would know that a D+ is not the basis for ending one's life. With these other data points, you would find yourself "arguing" (at least in your head) about the conclusions she was drawing. In other words, your brain would automatically start to recognize the distortions and begin to reframe the event in a more realistic way.

This same process will happen if you write out a description of both the event that you are finding stressful as well as your interpretation (that voice going off in your head) of the situation. For example, imagine that the first person you ask to the prom turns you down. As you tune into what you are saying to yourself about this event, you pick up that you are interpreting it as evidence that you are a loser and that no one would want to go with you. If you identify that thought, which by the way would certainly be a very unhappy situation if it were true, you find that your brain starts to add contradictory data. You remember, for example, that so and so had already asked you, or that there were two other people you thought about asking, or even that two of your friends had decided to go solo. These data directly confront the belief that you are a loser and that no one would go with you, thus bringing the event back into a more realistic (yes, disappointing but realistic) perspective. Using a six-column method of debating and reworking irrational, catastrophic thoughts is a good way to become a better manager of stress (see Your Turn 8.2).

YOUR TURN 8.2

Using the Six-Column Method

Directions: In order to learn to identify your catastrophic thinking and rework it so that your reactions to stress are more functional, it is helpful to maintain a log in which you can challenge beliefs. Use the example as your guide.

Event	Consequences	Beliefs (my self-talk and interpretations)	My Debating	My Reframing; My Interpretation	New Consequences
I had my first car accident. I'm not hurt, but broke my headlight and dented the right fender.	Terrified	Oh my god, my dad will kill me. I will never be allowed to drive again.	Wait . . . when has he reacted with violence? Even if he doesn't allow me to drive, someday I'll be on my own. How has he reacted when I've broken things in the past?	My dad is going to be upset . . . most likely. He will be happy I'm not hurt. I will probably have to pay for the repairs.	Moderately anxious about telling Dad and disappointed this will cost me.

Identify the (Realistic) Worst-Case Scenario

One final strategy that can help when feeling overwhelmed with stress is to identify the worst-case scenario. Rather than trying to convince yourself that everything will be okay (and it might be), it is sometimes helpful to attempt to identify the realistic worst case.

Okay, so let's imagine you get rejected from every college to which you applied. What are the probable consequences that are based in reality? Perhaps it means that you will have to delay starting college until you can apply to other colleges. Perhaps it means you will need to rethink going to college and consider a trade school or a certificate program. Or it may mean that you now have time to work and make some money for school. While being rejected is disappointing, it truly is not the end of the world, nor is it even the end of your progress toward your degree or career. Knowing this will help you not only resist catastrophizing but will also direct you to considering strategies that will move you forward.

8.7: The Take Away

- Stress is our reaction to life events that require adjustment and adaptation.

- A major contributor to one's experience of stress is the perception of the event associated with the stress.

- Our emotional and behavioral reactions to stress are mediated by our interpretation of and meaning given to life events.

- Humans have the ability to engage in reasonable, rational assessment of life events and in so doing keep the stress experienced proportional to the actual demands encountered.

- Humans have the ability to engage in distorted, irrational, catastrophic thinking which results in magnification of the experienced life event and a maximization of the stress experienced.

- There are a number of strategies that can help an individual de-catastrophize a situation and thus effectively adjust to the stress. These include things such as 1) approaching life events with the mindset of a scientist–researcher, 2) writing down concerns and specific elements of the demands encountered, and 3) identifying and preparing responses to a realistic "worst-case scenario."

CAN'T IGNORE THE BODY

"SO ... BREEEEEEATHHHE!"

The coach is like a maniac. Every practice we each shoot 15 foul shots and all the time he's hollering "breeeeeeathhhe." He says if we take slow, smooth breaths before a shot it calms us.

It sounds to us that the coach knows a little bit about stress, its effects on the body, and the way to use the body to calm and reduce stress.

While we have emphasized the role that your thinking plays in the creation and management of stress, we cannot ignore the body's contributions to one's vulnerability to stress as well as one's management of stress.

We are sure that this is not NEWS. It is, however, worth repeating. To manage stress you need to take good care of yourself. Take care of your body. You know, eat properly, get your rest, exercise, etc., etc.

The problem is that while you and most of us know this, we too often fail to do this. But really, it's time to get serious about all of this. We know in the short term stress interferes with our happiness and our effectiveness; in the long run, it will harm us, even kill us. So it is time to reduce our vulnerability to stress and learn to engage in those activities that increase our resistance and our resilience in the face of stress.

9.1: Taking Care of Your Body— Reducing Stress Vulnerability

Where to begin? Well it is best to start with the basics. In order to reduce your vulnerability to stress and the negative impacts of stress, you will need to reconsider your nutritional habits, your engagement in exercise, and even your sleep habits. It's a lot to do and you don't have to do it all at once. Even small steps towards a healthier lifestyle taken in any or all of these areas can make a significant difference.

Nutrition

The data are all too clear. Poor nutrition contributes to stress, fatigue, and will, over time, result in major health concerns including heart disease, stroke, type-2 diabetes, osteoporosis, even some cancers. Healthy eating is not simply a good idea, it is an essential practice if you are going to navigate the many demands of life you will encounter. Sounds reasonable and easy enough? It is if you live in a bubble. But as evidenced by Josh's experience (see Voices From Campus 9.1), the campus may not be the best place to begin to develop healthy eating habits.

VOICES FROM CAMPUS 9.1

Josh and the Freshman 15

Okay, so I'm what you could call "big boned." I played football in high school and was a solid 6'3", 218 pounds. Throughout my elementary, middle, and high school years I was always involved in sports and very conscious (especially once I hit my teens) about proper nutrition and working out. You know—I had those dreams of the NFL.

Well, when I decided to go to a division I-A school I soon realized that my football talents would not survive with these monsters. I continued to play intramural sports and generally focused on my studies. All good.

Things went well my freshman year. Lots of new friends, lots of new experiences, lots of fun ... and lots of pounds. I heard about the freshman 15 (that is gaining 15 lbs.), and well, I look to do things right. So by the winter break I was up to 238 pounds and found myself wearing sweats all day.

It was simply too easy to eat too much and too much of the wrong thing. We would study at 10 o'clock at night and be chowing down on pizza, fries, and barrels of coke. Breakfast started off okay ... you know, I would grab some fruit, eggs, maybe bacon. But then I would sit there and my friends would trickle in, so why not grab some chocolate milk maybe a donut or some pastries. You know, be sociable.

Well this pattern would continue at lunch and dinner times. After all, so many options, all you can eat, and sitting with friends. It became a graze fest.

Not only did I no longer fit into my pants, but I also felt like a slug and found myself tired and almost dozing off in class after eating all that sugar.

It's second semester and guess where I am? Back on campus ... in the gym ... and walking away from that dessert station. It's tough but I'm committed to gettin' down to my 218 or at least back into my pants.

Now with all of the things on your "to do" list, revamping your eating preferences may not be high on that list. Even so there are a few small things you can do that will, over time, have big payoffs. But before we think about this, let's take a little inventory of where you stand (see Your Turn 9.1).

YOUR TURN 9.1

A Snapshot of Where I Stand (Nutritionally)

Directions: Below you will find a very elementary breakdown of healthy versus unhealthy foods. Clearly the term unhealthy needs to be viewed as a relative term; it really depends on quantity and frequency. But your task is to place an "X" along each continuum as a way of developing your eating profile. In completing this scale, use the past seven days as your focus and data. Do you see areas where your nutritional profile could be improved?

Category	Healthy—examples (4)	(3)	(2)	Unhealthy—examples (1)
Dairy	Fat-free or low-fat milk Low-fat or reduced-fat cheeses Fat-free or low-fat Greek style yogurt Fat-free or light cream cheese			Whole milk Chocolate/strawberry milk Ice cream Heavy cream Processed cheeses
Cereals Crackers Rice Noodles Pasta	Oatmeal Brown rice Quinoa			White rice Sugar-coated cereals (e.g., Fruit Loops, Captain Crunch, etc.)
Vegetables	Fresh veggies, steamed veggies			No veggies

Category	Healthy—examples (4)	(3)	(2)	Unhealthy—examples (1)
Breads Muffins Rolls	Whole-grain bread Bagels English muffins Pita bread			Pastries Donuts White bread Corn bread
Nuts and seeds	Almonds Unsalted mixed nuts Unsalted sesame seeds Pumpkin seeds Sunflower seeds			Cracker jacks Salted nuts Honey-coated nuts Beer nuts Sweet and crunchy peanuts
Meat Fish Poultry	White meat chicken or turkey (skin off) Fish (not battered) Beef, round or sirloin			Fried chicken Fried fish Lunch meats Hot dogs Bacon
Fruit	Any fresh fruit 100% fruit juice			Fruit juice with sugar added (those little boxes) Canned fruit, sugar added
Beverages	Coffee Assorted teas Carbonated water Water			Soda Smoothies Fruit drinks Sports drinks
Preparation	Freshly prepared whole foods			Processed and fast food (e.g., pizza, burgers, hoagies, subs, etc.)

Perhaps upon reflection you discovered you are doing quite well when it comes to managing your nutritional needs. We hope that continues. And while we hope it does, we are also very mindful of the temptations and challenges that await you on campus (remember Josh, Voices From Campus 9.1).

On campus there will be unlimited availability of fast foods late into the evening, and desserts or sweets at every meal. The sodas are there for the tapping, as are coffee, hot chocolate, and fruit drinks. Now don't get us wrong, college officials are aware of the importance of nutrition and will provide many highly nutritional alternatives, but the choice is yours and the temptation is strong. So even if you are doing well, you may want to consider embracing one or more of the following as a beacon to guide your selections.

- *Increase meal frequency while reducing amounts.* Get into the habit of eating more frequent, smaller meals, especially during those days of high demand and thus high stress, the frequency will help stabilize your sugar levels smoothing out the highs and lows.
- *Eat breakfast.* It's often a hassle, especially when running late. But eating breakfast will kick-start your metabolism and again stabilize your blood sugar thus reducing stress. WARNING! Donuts don't count as breakfast, at least not a healthy breakfast. Try whole-grain cereal, oatmeal, protein, and fresh fruit.
- *Ingest stress busters.* Increase your intake of foods high in vitamin B (e.g., dairy, fish, leafy greens, bananas, meat) and vitamin C (e.g., citrus fruit, broccoli, kiwi, tomatoes). They are all stress busters. To ease anxiety and relax muscles, ingest foods that increase magnesium intake, such as nuts, rice, and beans.
- *Down with the caffeine.* Okay, bummer. But the lift you get from caffeine really has negative effects on the body when overdone, so MODERATION!!! Begin substituting your caffeinated drinks with herbal tea, green tea, or water.
- *Out with sugar.* Since we are attacking on all fronts. Try to reduce the amount of sugar, especially soft drinks, you ingest and switch to sparkling water.
- *Alcohol* ... Do we need to say anything?

We are not suggesting you become a purist, but take time to care for yourself and your body. Small modifications and moderation will show dividends almost immediately. Think about it. Have you ever participated in the Easter Bunny binge or Halloween bust, where you cleared all the candy from the bowl? Next day? Headache? Fatigue? Ridiculous cravings? Not real motivated to do much of anything except lay around? Yep, that is the wonderful effect of too much sugar, too much fat, too many empty calories on our system. So moderation is important if you are indulging with items that can contribute to stress.

Exercise

Want to blow off steam? How about release stress and tension? Well then, EXERCISE!

Yep, studies have shown that moderate exercise can not only relieve stress but also improve cognitive functioning (see "Stress and Exercise" from the American Psychological Association at www.apa.org/news/press/releases/stress/2013/exercise.aspx). The actual mechanism by which exercise reduces stress is not completely clear. It is believed that exercise stimulates the neuromodulator norepinephrine, which in turn may help the brain deal with stress more efficiently. Others suggest that exercise really provides the body a chance to practice dealing with stress since it forces our various physiological systems (e.g., cardiovascular, muscular, etc.) to coordinate and work more effectively together. Whatever the mechanism the research is clear: exercise helps us to effectively respond to and manage stress.

Now for many of us the very word "exercise" brings a slight wave of terror. I mean, who wants to get up at 5 a.m. to run 10 miles? Or how thrilled are you thinking about going to the gym to sweat and grunt for an hour?

Well actually, there are a lot of people who do really enjoy exercise and you may be one. But for those who are less inclined, even some exercise in a moderate form can still be within reach and of value.

If exercise is not really your thing, then consider trying moderate aerobic activities such as biking, walking, dancing, or, if possible, swimming. These require little equipment and often can be done while socializing. Or if you prefer, it is helpful to simply be mindful of the value of exercise and arrange your daily activities in ways that maximize your anaerobic capabilities. For example, when parking on campus or at the mall, select a spot at the extreme end of the lot. When going to your class, use the steps rather than the elevator. You may even begin to get tricky and take two steps at a time. And even when you are in the dining hall, rather than getting all your courses at one time, force yourself to walk back for additional courses or more to drink. Little things like these modest adjustments can have a meaningful impact.

Sleep

Take a good look around campus, especially around midterm or final exam times, and you will swear you are on the scene of a zombie movie.

Sleep? If you are like most students entering or in college, you're thinking, "I'll sleep someday." I mean you have projects, papers, tests … oh, and video games and television and social media and … parties (okay gatherings).

In other words, there is so much to do and so little time why waste it on sleep?

Well, as you may already have experienced, skipping sleep while engaging in so much is like burning your candle at both ends. Somewhere along the line your wicks will be shot. There is simply too much research evidence that shows that sleep deprivation results in increased irritability, disruption in our ability to concentrate and pay attention, as well as a reduction in our creativity, for us to ignore these ill effects. Further, and core to our discussion, the lack of sleep increases one's susceptibility to stress and conditions including depression and anxiety. And the effects of sleep deprivation are quick. For example, the researchers at the University of Pennsylvania reported that even partial sleep deprivation (i.e., sleeping 4.5 hours a night for one week) resulted in feeling more stressed, angry, sad, and mentally exhausted. The good news? These same researchers found that once a healthy sleep pattern was experienced, the negative effects disappeared.

So surrendering our sleep time is not a wise or productive thing to do. And while we know this, we also know that surrendering sleep in order to engage in campus life is truly a norm on most college campuses. So before we suggest some things that could help you develop a healthy sleep pattern we invite you to assess how you are currently doing. Your Turn 9.2 invites you to take the Epworth Sleepiness Scale.

YOUR TURN 9.2

The Epworth Sleepiness Scale

Directions: The Epworth Sleepiness Scale was developed in the 1990s and continues to be used today to assess levels of daytime sleepiness. Go to the following website to take the test http://www.skillsyouneed.com/ls/index .php/454661/.

Well, how did you do? Sleepy???

If you think adjusting your sleep pattern is worthwhile, we have a few suggestions that may help. Now, as with other ways of reducing stress vulnerability, you don't need to do a massive, all-inclusive overhaul of your sleep patterns. Rather, it would be helpful to identify those areas where maybe you have been negligent and focus your attention on changing those things.

- *Routine.* Researchers have found that establishing a time for bed and a time to wake as a routine seems to help us to more rapidly get to sleep and stay asleep.

- *Quiet, please.* We know the reality of dorm life, shared apartment living, and even being at home with others in the house, BUT as much as possible, reduce the noise pollution. While you may not be able to quiet the dorm, you may want to consider very inexpensive ear plugs that you can get at most pharmacies. Or if possible, employ white noise or a constant ambient sound that helps mask outside noise.

- *Be cool.* Many sleep experts say that a cool room, somewhere around 65 degrees, makes for the best sleep. Now with each of these suggestions you need to be in tune with your own preferences, so you may have to experiment in order to find the optimal temperature.

- *Bed and bedtime for sleeping.* It is important to develop the expectation that bed is the trigger for sleeping. As such, it is not a good idea to read in bed or watch television, and certainly it is not conducive for sleeping to use your bed as the staging for playing video games. Do these while sitting in a chair or on the floor and use the bed for sleeping.

- *Relax.* Sometimes the pace of the day may make it difficult to relax prior to sleep. Try taking a warm bath or shower.

- *DON'T.* While it is obvious ... stay away from caffeine, alcohol, or big meals at least a couple of hours before sleeping.

Now while each of the above is a good suggestion, sleep experts have noted that most people will have a difficult time following all. Our suggestion is simply to start with one or two and try to incorporate those into your routine. Identify the pattern that is disrupting your sleep and try to address it. It may be as simple as committing to watching television from a chair or reading at your desk and keeping the bed for sleeping.

9.2: The Simple Act of Breathing—A Major Stress Buster

While attempting to change our lifestyles and habits is a good way to reduce our vulnerability to stress, there are times when stress has engulfed us and we need to intervene. As the coach to whom we referred in our opening reflection most aptly noted, the intervention needed at times of stress may be as simple as … breeeeeeathhhe. But it is not that simple inhale, exhale pattern we associate with typical breathing. Breathing as a stress buster has a unique form.

Have you ever observed little children who are upset and crying? Watch how they breathe. It is very spastic. They are taking short, choppy breaths often very rapid and shallow and coming from the chest. This is neither an indication that they are relaxed nor is it the type of breathing that induces relaxation. This is stressed breathing.

Now watch those same children sleeping. Now the breathing is smooth, not choppy; rhythmic rather than spastic; slow and deep rather than short and shallow; and most often the breathing is diaphragmatic, engaging the area above the belly.

When we are engaged in this type of breathing, our stress is reduced. It has to be! We can't breathe like this if we are in flight or fight mode. So placing our attention on eliciting this type of behavior will engage our quieting or relaxing response and thus serve as a wonderful tool for reducing and managing stress.

While there are numerous ways to learn to engage in this type of breathing, a very simple exercise is found in Your Turn 9.3. We suggest you practice it, and practice it regularly. Make it part of your normal repertoire. With practice it can become almost automatic and can serve you well as a stress buster.

YOUR TURN 9.3

The Quieting Response—Breathing for Relaxation

Directions: This is a very simple exercise and yet a very powerful tool and intervention. The more you practice, the more automatic this will become. In fact, you may want to identify triggers for practice. For example, when you end a phone call or when a particular television show goes off or even at red lights (just don't get too relaxed) you could try to get into the smooth, slow, rhythmic breathing described below.

Step 1: Get into a comfortable position, preferably sitting, not lying down.

Step 2: Exhale completely through your mouth. It is okay to make a sound.

Step 3: Close your mouth and inhale through your nose. When comfortable with the rate of intake (some breathe in faster than others), mentally count to four to see if you can begin to establish a rhythm.

Step 4: Pause. In an attempt to develop a smooth rhythm, it is helpful to pause very slightly, prior to exhaling and similarly prior to inhaling on the next breath. It may help to imagine that your breath is like a long rope swing that, when it begins to reverse its direction, pauses slightly (not a stop or major hesitation, just a pause) as it reverses.

Step 5: Exhale. Exhale through your mouth at a speed that is comfortable. The goal is to make the inhaling and exhaling a smooth rhythmic process (like the swing back and forth). We are attempting to make the intake rhythm match the exhale rhythm. So see if you can exhale to a four count. If that is too slow, then make it a three count. But try to get it as slow as possible while staying rhythmic.

Step 6: Now repeat this cycle. As you do, mentally say to yourself, "SLOW, SMOOTH, RHYTHMIC breaths."

With practice you will be able to get into the rhythm faster and will be able to slow the exchange. You will find that this is useful at times of stress (even when shooting that foul shot) and can be used as an aid to falling asleep.

9.3: The Take Away

- To manage stress, you need to take good care of yourself. Take care of your body.

- Poor nutrition contributes to stress, fatigue, and will, over time, result in major health concerns including heart disease, stroke, type-2 diabetes, osteoporosis, even some cancers.

- It is valuable to eat small and frequent meals of freshly prepared foods and avoid the processed, sugary foods so readily available.

- Moderate exercise can not only relieve stress but also improve cognitive functioning.

- It can help to simply be mindful of the value of exercise and arrange your daily activities in ways that maximize your anaerobic capabilities.

- The effects of sleep deprivation are quick, and even one week of sleep deprivation (4.5 hours of sleep a night) can result in feeling more stressed, angry, sad, and mentally exhausted.

- It is valuable to develop a sleep-time routine including time to bed and time to wake. Do so in a cool, quiet environment (even if it takes ear plugs or white noise).

- The quieting response of slow, smooth, rhythmic breathing is one of the best stress busters we have. It needs to be developed, practiced, and become a part of your automatic response to stressful situations.

CHAPTER 10

YOU NEED A FRIEND OR TWO: CONNECTING AND NETWORKING

This college campus is really huge! I have no clue if anyone else from my high school is around. It's weird without the old group.

T here is much to think about when you first get to college. Getting settled in your dorm or accustomed to your commute, understanding your schedule, and managing your money are tasks which can be very challenging. Two strategies that can be quite helpful to not only decrease the stress of adapting to college life but also make your college career an enriching and successful one are *connecting* and *networking*.

Some of you will look forward to meeting new people every day and others of you will find a group of peers and be happy hanging with just them. You may find a group that serves both as a source of friends and professional connections, or you may have different groups for each. Whatever works for you, being socially and professionally connected in college can help your college experience be more meaningful and even happier. Why?

These social connections act as support and opportunities for fun and enjoyment. But beyond the obvious, networking will open new doors and new associations for personal and professional growth. As you meet more people, you increase the possibility for additional opportunities in college and even after graduation. The value of networking and connecting can be seen in the experiences shared by two college students in the following stories in Voices From Campus 10.1.

VOICES FROM CAMPUS 10.1

Ariel

I was really anxious about getting everything done and getting good grades during my college years. I studied alone and when my room-mate asked me to join her, I rarely did. I concentrated solely on my work and didn't think I had the time to join any clubs or organizations. When my classmates would talk about activities they had done and events they had been to, they sounded interesting, but I didn't want to be distracted from my work, so I never went.

Now that I'm in my last semester and getting ready to gradu-ate, I have a great GPA, but I'm kinda worried about getting a job. My roommate and most of my classmates are talking about their internship experiences and all the activities they're putting on their résumés. Some of them have even received job offers and said that somebody they knew put in a good word for them when they ap-plied. I'm starting to regret not being better connected with people and organizations in college. And why didn't I go to the career center earlier? I'll make an appointment today, but I think it's kinda late ...

Troy

There was a lot going on when I started college my freshman year. So many things to do and so much to think about doing! I knew I had to get used to studying and working on my assignments, but when there was an event for my major, I went, and boy am I glad I did! The Big Brothers, Big Sisters event was a great opportunity to learn more about working with kids with special needs, but more than that, I got to meet so many other students and faculty who were involved with these kids. It turned out to be a great experience for my future work as a special education teacher. Not only that, one of the faculty members was doing research on students with disabilities and the use of therapy pets—how cool is that?! I was really interested in that and I was able to help with the research.

As I'm getting ready to graduate, I am so excited to start my career and think I have had some unbelievable experiences in college. I don't know what I would have done without my friends who will now be my teaching colleagues. I know we'll stay in touch so we can continue to bounce ideas off of each other, and keep each other sane!

10.1: Connecting

Ariel and Troy had very different experiences in college, and although both were concerned with being good students, Troy's time at college was enriched through his connections with peers and professors. His experiences enabled him to grow professionally and to feel excited to start his career. It is not only in the classroom that meaningful learning takes place, nor is it always at organized gatherings where social needs are met. We invite you to reflect about the types of experiences you think will be valuable for your time at college, both personally and professionally, in Your Turn 10.1.

YOUR TURN 10.1

Making Your College Experience Count

Directions: Reflect on the types of experiences that you believe will be valuable to you personally and professionally during your time in college.

What type of experience do I desire?	What to investigate?	Personal benefit?	Professional benefit?
Activities connected to my field of study	Professional organizations Service clubs Research with faculty Internships		

Service to community	University volunteer Community event volunteer		
Specific focus groups	Fraternity or sorority Resident life group Commuter group		
Physical activities	Intramural league Sports clubs		
Other			

It is very likely that when you started the search for possible colleges to attend you read a lot about their academic reputation, their tuition and fees, and the specific majors they offered. That is essential. But expanding your knowledge of the resources available to you once on campus is also essential. It would be useful for you to visit the college website and see what is available in the student life or student engagement areas. Typically colleges provide multiple opportunities for social engagement and student interaction. Hopefully you will see some clubs, organizations, or activities that meet your needs. But even if you don't find something that attracts you, you may find that your campus allows you to form your own interest group! Of course all of your connections don't have to be so organized or formal. You can start or join in a study group, coffee gathering, or any of your various interests from "video gaming" to social activism. Trust us, you are not the only one with those interests, so reach out. There will be a lot of people around you; find a connection!

Beyond the peer-social connections, it is important to be aware of the resources available on campus and connect with them. Think about where you may have gone for advice or support in the past. While in high school, you may have met with your school counselor for advisement regarding course selection, and you may have attended a Financial Aid Night to find out about college loans. Or perhaps you had a church group or a youth minister that was a support at times of stress. It will be helpful to connect with someone regarding these types of things on a college campus, as well. Your academic advisor and financial aid office are just two of the connections you will want to make early in your college career. Remember, one of the ways to manage stress is to plan ahead and know when deadlines are coming! It's never too early to check out the career center or too soon to talk with your resident advisor if there is an issue at the dorm. Use the resources on campus; there will be many!

Okay, you are thinking about connecting to people, departments, resources, groups … but when, and how many, and …?!

This is supposed to be helpful, so let's take a minute to understand why you are doing all this connecting. Building connections with people and resources builds your support system. You may feel like you can wing it on your own, but we think that if you are like most, you will see the advantage of having others to guide you, to provide alternative perspectives, and even just let you blow off steam. But beyond this value, connecting in the form of networking can enhance your life after graduation.

10.2: Networking

For you, networking will be building a group of interconnected people, and in this case, these are people who can support you in your career. We know you are just starting out and we are talking about graduation and careers. But it is important to think about that even when starting out.

Connecting With Those in the Field or on Their Way

The more connected you are with other students and professionals in your field, the more information, knowledge, and experiences become available. Shellise West from San Jose State university posted "4 Reasons Why Networking in College Is Important" (see http://www.hercampus.com/school/sjsu/4-reasons-why-networking-college-important). She notes that networking is helpful in the following ways:

Knowledge—Very simply put, connecting with those working in the field or students who may be further along in the same major as you provides resources to begin to understand the reality (both good and bad) of the career that you may be pursuing.

Advice—The advice given from your prospective networking connections can help you become familiar with what to do and what not to do when it comes to your potential career. Speaking to those within your major who are completing their studies is a great way to identify the things they would have done differently and would be useful for you to do.

Referrals—Referrals are critical for students looking to work in their chosen fields.

Job Opportunities—Along with receiving a referral letter, networking can most importantly supply you with a job in your future.

Connecting for a Broader Perspective

In addition to gaining the perspective of those in or about to enter your field, it is helpful to gain a broader perspective on careers, job opportunities, and life after college. Your college career center is a resource that not only helps with career development, but is also a great source to help you with networking! The career center may be helpful in connecting you with alumni in your field and opportunities for internships, and then eventual employment. And while it may seem like a lot of work, developing a list of possible resources and connections from your past, those to whom you could turn for support throughout your program and eventual employment, is something you should begin right away. This would be a good time to make a list of your friends' parents, your parents' friends, your teachers, past employers, and anyone else you can think of who could be a part of your networking group. Don't forget to include events and other opportunities. The exercise found in Your Turn 10.2 can help get you started.

YOUR TURN 10.2

Starting a Networking List

Directions: Think of people and opportunities that may provide knowledge and advice for your career.

Who?	What will they provide?
People who hold the position you aspire to hold	Knowledge Advice Shadowing/internship possibilities
People who are just starting in the field, such as peers in your classes	Their perspective on information you're learning Ideas for networking
Parents, parents' friends, friends' parents	Job opportunities Identifying your strengths Personal references
Teachers	Advice Identifying your strengths

Employers	Professional references Job opportunities
Conferences	
Job fairs	
Career counselors or centers	
Other	

One last word regarding networking, and it's a word of caution. Actually, there are two words: social media.

Obviously you understand and have experienced social media as a way to connect with others. You may even realize that social media can serve as a resource for information and notifications about job possibilities. When used in these ways it can be a wonderful tool. But it is very ... let's repeat ... very important that you realize gaining information by way of social media is a two-way street.

Potential employers may use social media to learn about you. Think about that for a moment. Think about the information you have posted, or that perhaps someone else has posted about you. Are there pictures that you may be hesitant to show your parents? If so, how do you feel they would serve you if they were considered as part of your job intake information?

So please make sure any information about you that is posted on the Internet and social media is information that will help you gain employment! Make sure that the image and data presented places you within the best context, highlighting your social skills, your talents, and your strengths, especially those that would make you an appealing candidate and employee. Take a look at Voices From Campus 10.2 and consider which scenario would be more valuable in your job search.

VOICES FROM CAMPUS 10.2

Scenario 1 (Kyle)

I hope that was the worst interview I will ever have! I can't believe that guy asked me if I posted stuff on social media sites. Who doesn't post stuff? What difference does it make if I have pictures of my friends and me having a good time doing keg stands? I mean, at least it shows I'm personable and agile. If I have a high GPA and great reference letters, that's all that matters for a job, right? Okay, so he said it would have helped if I knew more about this entry position and what was expected of me. How am I supposed to know until I start? Isn't he the one who is supposed to tell me what I'm supposed to know? I don't think I'll be hearing back from him.

Scenario 2 (Jessie)

I am so glad I talked to Dr. John and Mrs. Lane about what this job might entail. The human resource director was so impressed with my questions! She said my internships and summer work really moved me up the list of candidates. And she was really happy when I told her I don't have a personal account in social media. She was so interested in my leadership role I held in the service organization in college. I think she might have belonged to the same one! I think I have a really good chance at getting this job!

10.3: The Take Away

- College can offer many opportunities to meet new people for personal and social connections and for professional connections.

- There are clubs and organizations for a vast array of interests—check out your college website or office of student engagement.

- Connections with people and resources can provide support and information, and fun experiences!

- Knowledge, advice, references, and possible job opportunities are some of the benefits that may come out of networking.

- Networking in college can provide you with greater opportunities for interviews and jobs!

- What you put on the Web … is for the world to see. Think about who might see it and what impact it can have on your future career.

BIBLIOGRAPHY

Anspaugh, D. J. Hamrick, M., & Rosato, F. et al. (2011). Coping with and managing stress. In *Wellness: Concepts and applications* (8th ed.), (pp. 307–340). New York: McGraw-Hill.

Broderick, P. (2013). *Learning to breathe: A mindfulness curriculum for adolescents to cultivate emotion regulation, attention, and performance.* Oakland, CA: New Harbinger Publications, Inc.

Center for Collegiate Mental Health (2016). *Annual report, 2016.* Retrieved from http://ccmh.psu.edu/publications/

Crum, A. J., Salovey, P., & Achor, S. (2013). Rethinking stress: The role of mindsets in determining the stress response. *Journal of Personality and Social Psychology, 104*(4), 716–733.

Davis, M. (2000). *The relaxation and stress reduction workbook.* Oakland, CA: New Harbinger Inc.

Denollet, J., Schiffer, A., & Spek, V. (2010). A general propensity to psychological distress affects cardiovascular outcomes: Evidence from research on the type D (distressed) personality profile. *Circulation: Cardiovascular Quality and Outcomes, 3,* 546–557.

Dinges, D., Pack, F., Williams, K., Gillen, K., Powell, J., Ott, G., Aptowicz, C., & Pack, A. (1997). Cumulative sleepiness, mood disturbance, and psychomotor vigilance decrements during a week of sleep restricted to 4–5 hours per night. *Sleep, 20*(4), 267–277.

Fisher, R., Ury, W. L., & Patton, B. (2011). *Getting to Yes: Negotiating agreement without giving in.* New York, NY: Penguin Books.

Grossman, P., Niemann, L., Schmidt, S., & Walach, H. (2004). Mindfulness-based stress reduction and health benefits. *Journal of Psychosomatic Research, 57*(1), 35–43.

Harvey, A. G., & Bryant, R. A. (2002). Acute stress disorder: A synthesis and critique. *Psychological Bulletin, 128,* 886–902.

Kohn, P. M., Lafreniere, K., & Gurevich, M. (1990). The Inventory of College Students' Recent Life Experiences: A decontaminated hassles scale for a special population. *Journal of Behavioral Medicine, 13*(6), 619–630.

Lazarus, R. S. (1999). *Stress and emotion: A new synthesis.* New York: Springer.

Lewis, D. (2004). *Free your breath, free your life: Conscious breathing can relieve stress, increase vitality, and help you live more fully.* Boston: Shambala Publications.

Linden, W. (2005). *Stress management: From basic science to better practice.* Thousand Oaks, CA: SAGE Publications.

Murray, M. T. (2013). Stress management. In J. E. Pizzorno & M. T. Murray (Eds.), *Textbook of natural medicine,* 4th ed. (pp. 547–554). St. Louis: Mosby.

Nelson, D., & Cooper, C. (2005). Stress and health: A positive direction. *Stress and Health, 21*(2), 73–75.

Princeton Review (2016). *College hopes and worries survey, 2016.* Retrieved from https://www.google.com/search?client=safari&rls=en&q=Princeton+Review+College+Hopes+and+Worries+Survey+2016&ie=UTF-8&oe=UTF-8

Schneiderman, N., Ironson, G., & Siegel, S. D. (2005). Stress and health: Psychological, behavioral and biological determinants. *Annual Review Clinical Psychology, 1,* 607–628.

Schiraldi, G. R. (2016). *Stress management strategies.* Dubuque, IA: Kendall/Hunt Publishing Company.

Smyth, J., Zawadzki, M., & Gerin, W. (2013). Stress and disease: A structural and functional analysis. *Social and Personality Psychology Compass, 7,* 217–227.

Todd, J., & Mullan, B. (2014). The role of self-monitoring and response inhibition in improving sleep behaviours. *International Journal of Behavioral Medicine, 21*(3), 470–477.

Tovian, S., Thorn, B., Coons, H., Labott, S., Burg, M., Surwit, R., & Bruns, D. (n.d.). *Stress effects on the body.* Retrieved from http://www.apa.org/helpcenter/stress-body.aspx.

APPENDIX

WHERE TO TURN— ADDITIONAL RESOURCES

In Print

Biegel, G. M. (2009). *The Stress Reduction Workbook for Teens: Mindfulness Skills to Help You Deal with Stress.* Oakland, CA: New Harbinger Publications, Inc.

Davis, M. (2000). *The Relaxation and Stress Reduction Workbook.* Oakland, CA: New Harbinger Publications, Inc.

Reber, D. (2008). *Chill: Stress-Reducing Techniques for a More Balanced, Peaceful You.* New York, NY: Simon Pulse.

Rossman, M. (2010). *The Worry Solution: Using Breakthrough Brain Science to Turn Stress and Anxiety into Confidence and Happiness.* New York, NY: Harmony.

Sood, A. (2013). *The Mayo Clinic Guide to Stress-Free Living.* Philadelphia, PA: DeCapo Press.

Weller, S. (2000). *The Breath Book: 20 Ways to Breathe Away Stress, Anxiety and Fatigue.* London, England: Thorsons.

Wilson, R., & Branch, R. (2005). *Cognitive Behavioural Therapy for Dummies.* Chichester, West Sussex, England: John Wiley & Sons, Ltd.

On the Web

Doyle, A. (2016). Top 10 career networking tips for college students. https://www.thebalance.com/top-career-networking-tips-for-college-students-2062581

Grant, A. (2011). 6 ways to network while you're in college. https://www.usnews.com/education/best-colleges/articles/2011/09/28/6-ways-to-network-while-youre-in-college Grohol, J. M. (2017). Stress management: Coping with stress. http://psychcentral.com/stress/

Mills, H., Reiss, N., & Dombeck, M. (n.d.). Stress reduction and management: Cognitive restructuring. http://www.gulfbend.org/poc/view_doc.php?type=doc&id=15670&cn=117

The Centre for Cognitive-Behavioral Therapy. http://www.centreforcbtcounselling.co.uk/stress.php